HEIRS WITH
THE PRINCE

HEIRS WITH THE PRINCE

Stephen Brown

Thomas Nelson Publishers
Nashville • Camden • New York

Published in Nashville, Tennessee, by Thomas Nelson, Inc., and distributed in Canada by Lawson Falle, Ltd., Cambridge, Ontario.

Printed in the United States of America.

Unless otherwise noted, the Bible version used in this publication is the New American Standard Bible, Copyright © The Lockman Foundation 1960, 1962, 1963, 1968, 1971, 1972, 1973, 1977, and is used by permission.

Those verses marked NIV are quoted from the New International Version, copyright © 1978 by the New York International Bible Society, and are used by permission.

Excerpts from *The Singer*, by Calvin Miller, Copyright © 1975, Inter-Varsity Fellowship of the USA, are used by permission of InterVarsity Press, Downers Grove, IL 60515.

"Lord, It Is Dark," is taken from *Prayers*, by Michel Quoist. Copyright © 1963, Sheed and Ward, Inc. Reprinted with permission of Andrews, McMeel, and Parker. All rights reserved.

ISBN 0-8407-5939-8

Contents

If you don't like this book, please remember that it could have been worse were it not for...

the love, advice, and support of my wife, Anna,

the patience of our two daughters, Robin and Jennifer,

the hours of correction and typing by my administrative assistant, Cathy Wyatt,

the advice of my associate, Dave O'Dowd,

the encouragement and prayers of the officers, staff, and members of the Key Biscayne Presbyterian Church, and

the gifted and sensitive editorial work by Larry Weeden.

...but then again, maybe it could have been better.

Introduction

When I left commercial broadcasting to attend seminary, Jon Holiday, the owner of the station for which I worked, called me into his office and said, "Steve, I want to wish you the best of luck, but I want to give you some advice. There is nothing wrong with making a mistake, but it is stupid to make the same mistake over and over again after you know it is a mistake."

I listened, wondering what he was trying to say. He continued: "Steve, I believe you are making a mistake with this seminary thing, and I'm afraid that you will be afraid to admit you were wrong. I just wanted you to know that when you realize your mistake, there will be a job waiting for you here. You are young and you are entitled to a few blunders, but when you realize that this is a blunder, you come on back to work for me. You are just too practical and realistic to be a minister."

I have often thought about Jon Holiday's words on that occasion, and through the years I have come to see that his attitude reflects the feeling of a lot of folks about Christians in general and pastors in particular. Christianity is seen as a nice system of beliefs for impractical people. But when it comes down to real living, one must be practical, and the Christian faith simply won't do. Religion is okay for children and dreamers, but it simply won't work in drive-time traffic, in business, and in dealing with real problems.

This book's contention is that the Christian faith is not only practical, but it is practical because it is true. It is a world view that works because it reflects reality.

I am a Christian because the Christian faith is true. I believe in the Bible and the doctrines taught therein because I have determined that the Bible is true. The Christian faith doesn't always make me feel good; sometimes I wish I could still be a pagan; sometimes I wish I had never heard about Christ. But the problem with the truth is that once you have seen it, you can't unsee it. Not only that, but once you see truth, you can't act as if you didn't see it without slipping over into the world of the neurotic. Too many Christians, I believe, have seen the truth and then act as if they had not seen it. It is the particular neurosis of the Christian community. This malady has created the false impression that the Christian faith is impractical. It isn't, but like soap, it doesn't work unless it is used. A dirty world doesn't prove that soap doesn't work any more than impractical Christians prove that Christianity doesn't work.

Someone told the story about two balloonists who had become lost somewhere in France. For days they hovered in the clouds. Finally they managed to get the balloon down below the clouds. There was a man standing on the ground and they shouted down to him, "Hey! Could you tell us where we are?"

The man called back, "You are in a balloon."

With that the balloon ascended back into the clouds. One of the balloonists turned to the other and said, "He must be an accountant. The information is accurate, but it is useless."

Too often Christians have developed the same attitude about our faith. It is true, of course, but it doesn't make much difference.

The great need of our time is for Christians not only to see the truth of the Christian faith, but also to see and live the practical implications that flow directly from its truth. This book is about practical implications, and it is written for Jon Holiday and numerous others like him who think that Christians, and the faith they proclaim, are impractical. It is also written for those Christians who, without meaning to, have given Jon Holiday and the others a false impression of the reality of our lives.

The Bible says that the God of the universe has entered time and space. It tells us that God has incarnated Himself in a Jew by the name of Jesus. In fact, the central doctrine of the Christian faith is the doctrine of the incarnation. The question this book proposes to answer is not so much whether or not it happened (although we will address that issue), but, rather, what difference it makes in a practical way.

To put it another way, the King of the universe, the Sovereign Ruler of all that is, has sent His Son, the Prince (John 3:16), into the hinterlands of the kingdom. That, in itself, is amazing enough. Let me tell you something even more amazing: the Prince, with the permission of the Sovereign, has decided to share all of His heritage with the citizens of the hinterlands. Christians have become, as it were, heirs with the Prince. Our problem is that we have too often acted as if we were the pauper children of a beggar.

It is my prayer, Christian friend, that you will accept your heritage, that you will use it, that you will bask in it, that you will allow it to make you different—and, more than that, that you will praise the Sovereign for it.

The Spirit Himself bears witness with our spirit that we are children of God, and if children, heirs also, heirs of God and fellow-heirs with Christ. (Rom. 8:16–17)

1 HOW I MET THE PRINCE

If Jesus has come...
tell me.

I bow my knees before the Father,... that He would grant you, accord-
ing to the riches of His glory,... to know the love of Christ which sur-
passes knowledge.
                                                            Ephesians 3:14, 16, 19

This book is about Jesus, and I want you to know from the
outset that I can hardly be called an objective observer. It would
be easier for me to be an objective observer of my best friend or
even my wife. When you begin to know Him, there is something about Jesus that gets under your skin. You either love
Him or you hate Him; you either follow Him or you run from
Him; you either accept His truth or you reject His truth. But it
is very difficult to be neutral. I know because I tried.

I have always been around a church. My father didn't care
much for the church but my mother did, and what my mother
decided, my brother and I accepted. We just didn't have a
choice. On Sunday mornings we went to church. We prayed
each morning before leaving for school, and we listened when
Mother read the Bible.

I don't want you to get the wrong impression. My mother
was not the kind of Christian who prayed on her knees on Sunday and preyed on her neighbors the rest of the week. She was
(and is) a very earthy and practical follower of Christ. When my
brother and I came home from school, we were never sure
whom we would find at our dinner table. Mother had a way of

bringing wounded people into our home. If they were hungry, they would be fed; if they needed a friend, she was their friend; if they needed a defender, she would be their defender. And she did it all for Jesus' sake. If you are ever going to be hanging over a cliff and you need someone to hold the rope, you call my mother. You can be sure she won't look at the clouds or smell the flowers. She will hold the rope for Jesus' sake.

Someone has said that God doesn't have any grandchildren. That's true. Here's another truth: Jesus doesn't have any nephews. If He did, my mother's elder brother, Jesus, would have been a favorite uncle. It didn't work out that way. She knew Jesus, but the reality of His life and love is not transferable. You've got to get those things from Him, and you've got to do it yourself.

College was a time of doubt in my life. I found that I couldn't run my spiritual car on my mother's gasoline. I questioned everything I had ever been taught; I discarded the beliefs I had been given and decided to form my own. I decided to replace the "myths" of my short past with a more rational and sophisticated system that would be geared for the "real world." I got married, started working in commercial broadcasting—and registered for Boston University School of Theology.

I registered for a school of theology because I just couldn't get away from Jesus.

I eventually dropped out of seminary. There were financial problems and time problems. But the real reason I dropped out of the theological world of higher learning was that I just couldn't believe in the product. My wife was pregnant, I had a good job at a radio station in Boston, and I decided that, for a change, I would make an honest living.

During the months that followed, I was confused, empty, and afraid. Even the birth of our first daughter, Robin (and she was a wonderful gift from the Father), did not help the hurt. I walked the beaches of the South Shore on cold winter days asking questions that had plagued me for years: What am I doing here? Does my living make any difference? Where am I going?

Am I working just to make enough money to keep working? And then the most important question: Is there a God, and if there is, what difference does it make?

Albert Camus said that the only question with which a thinking man must deal is the question of suicide. I can understand that, and there were times when it was an attractive option for me. I can remember coming home to our apartment and standing at the door and wanting to cry. I had everything I could possibly want. I had a wonderful wife I loved and who loved me; I had a beautiful new daughter; I had a very good job with a great future. But it wasn't enough. I went back to seminary feeling that if there were no answers there, there were no answers.

During this whole time I felt I was being "watched." The Watcher never spoke. He just watched silently and, though I didn't know it, lovingly. Everywhere I turned I met people who knew Him and loved Him: the afternoon disk jockey at the station where I was the morning host, the pastor who recorded his Sunday afternoon religious program during my assigned production time, the waitress in the coffee shop downstairs, my wife's obstetrician. They all knew the Watcher, and they talked about Him most of the time. The Watcher was Jesus, and I just couldn't get away from Him.

Don't misunderstand. I was not looking for Him. He was looking for me. He became the Watcher who was always there. I tried my best to ignore Him, but I couldn't. I tried to pretend, in my sophistication, that He didn't exist. I tried to turn away from any reality that didn't "fit" the reality I had created. In the fifth book of David Eddings's *Belgariad* series, General Varana, the Tolnedran, resolutely refused to believe in sorcery. He said, "It is a matter of principle, your Majesty. Tolnedrans do not believe in sorcery. I am a Tolnedran therefore I do not admit that it exists." Just at that moment a hawk landed in front of him and began to shimmer and change into a man. Eddings said of Varana, "General Varana resolutely turned his back and stared with apparently deep interest at the featureless hill some five miles distant."[1] Like Varana, I refused to confront any reality that disturbed my comfortable, nice, intellectual, little box. I was afraid that the Watcher really would be there and I would have to deal with Him and His demands on my life.

There were other times when I was just as afraid that He *wouldn't* be there and I would have to live with the resulting meaninglessness. Still, He watched silently, and I couldn't get away from Him. I was torn between my need for Him not to be there and my need for meaning that only He could provide.

Then our second daughter, Jennifer, was born, and in the midst of the joy and delight there was bad news. Jennifer had serious blood problems, and the doctor was afraid that one of her legs would not grow because it was not receiving proper nourishment. He said that once the blood count reached a certain level, Jennifer would be taken to Boston Children's Hospital for a complete blood transfusion. He mentioned the high mortality rate among children with this disorder and said, "I'm going to be perfectly honest with you, Mr. Brown. It isn't good."

A few weeks prior to Jennifer's birth, I had been introduced to some Christians who met each week for prayer, Bible study, and fellowship. I started going to those weekly meetings, not because I believed what they believed, but because it was nice to be around people who believed something. They had a warm spiritual fire, and I hovered on the cold fringes of their fire thinking about how nice it would be to be warm. The night of the day Jennifer was born, I went to those dear Christians to ask for their help. You need to I know that I would have gone to a witch doctor if a witch doctor could have helped. I didn't know a witch doctor; I only knew these Christians, so I went to them.

When I walked into the group, a number of them congratulated me on the birth of our new daughter. I don't generally talk about my problems, but that night I poured them all out. I told

---

1. David Eddings, *Enchanters' End Game* (New York: Ballantine Books, 1984), p. 202.

them how frightened and helpless I felt, and I told them how much I loved Jennifer, even if she was only a day old.

Those dear people didn't even talk about it; they immediately started praying. They prayed for me, and for my wife, Anna, and then they prayed for Jennifer. And they prayed in the name of the Watcher, Jesus.

The next day my wife, who was still in the hospital, called me from the hospital room. She didn't say "Good morning" or "How are you?" She said, "Honey, did anybody pray last night?" I told her about the prayers that were offered the night before. She said, "The doctor came in this morning very early and said, 'This is a miracle. The blood count is normal and I am no longer worried about the leg.' "

The day Jesus made my daughter well was one of the most significant days of my life. I had friends who knew Jesus whose babies had died; I knew godly people who had never seen a miracle; I was familiar with a lot of "unanswered prayer." The question was, "Why me? Why was *my* prayer answered?" It certainly was not because I was good, pure, kind, or spiritual. Jesus, the Watcher, had intervened in my life in a specific and clear way, and I just couldn't understand it. Later I was to realize that Jesus does a lot of things that are hard to understand, that He reaches out to people who don't deserve it.

The day Jennifer got well was the day of beginning in my life. For the next six years I asked questions of everyone I knew who knew Jesus. I read more books than I care to remember, and I prayed to the One who watched.

A friend of mine, Fred Smith, was with a group of men who had met for a weekend just to talk. Fred feels that one of the problems men have today is that they never get together just to get together. And so Fred often gets together a group of men for a weekend with no agenda. On this particular occasion, these men were meeting at a large ranch in Texas. One evening the subject of God came up in the conversation. Fred, who knows something about God, said that when God gets a man hooked that man ought to give up immediately, because if he struggles, all he does is get his blood in the water. Fred explained that when God hooks someone, He will reel him in.

Later that night when all the men were going back to their rooms, one man stopped Fred and said, "Fred, how do you know when you're hooked?" Fred replied that when it happens to someone he knows it.

The next day some of the men were walking around the ranch when the man to whom Fred had spoken the night before took off his clothes and jumped into one of the water holes on the ranch. It was a rather loose crowd, and no one paid any attention to the man. But at lunch that same man sat down by Fred and said, "You remember what you told me last night?" Fred replied that he did and the man went on, "Well, after I talked to you I decided I was hooked. I said to Him, 'I don't want to be a preacher, but if that's what You want, I'll be a darn good one.' "

"Did you wonder what I was doing this morning when I jumped into the water hole?" he asked.

"Yes," Fred replied, "but I figured it was your business."

"Well," the man said with a grin, "I baptized myself, because if you're hooked you ought to get baptized."

After six years of asking questions, reading books, and facing doubts, I was hooked. And I have been hooked ever since. Jesus is no longer the silent Watcher—in fact, He never was. I just wouldn't listen. At the end of the six years, I knelt down by the desk in my study and said, "I don't know everything about You, but I know enough to know that I want to know You better. I'm not much, but I am Yours. Do what You will with my life." He did, and my life has never been the same.

That experience was a long time ago; so long, in fact, that as I write this it seems as though I am talking about someone else. As I look back over the years, a lot of events aren't clear, but running through all of them is the reality of love and presence of Jesus. Lots of folks have lied to me, but He has never lied, not even once. A lot of people have failed me, and I have failed a lot of people, but He has never failed, not even once. I have never had to apologize for Him or criticize Him or be ashamed of

Him. He got under my skin and I can't get away from Him. Everywhere I turn, if I am quiet enough, I can hear the soft sound of His feet.

I have a friend who declared recently that he is an atheist. He has served as a pastor and a seminary teacher. He is the kind of person one does not expect to turn away from the faith. But he has. The interesting thing about my friend is that he denies God and the Bible and the church—but he can't bring himself to deny Jesus. When you ask him about Jesus he becomes strangely silent. I can understand that. I can understand it because I know how Jesus gets under your skin. He is sort of like a husband who has left his wife but remembers how much his wife loved him and how faithful she was. Whenever his former wife's name comes up in conversation, he changes the subject or grows silent. It's hard to get away from someone who loves you. Jesus' love is like that.

And so, don't expect me to be objective about Jesus. If I could, I would, but I can't. Further, to be perfectly honest with you, I can't see how anybody can be objective about Him. He doesn't allow objectivity. He forces Himself to be the issue, and then He calls for decision. In Matthew 16, there is a discussion between Jesus and His disciples. Jesus asked His disciples what people were saying about Him. They gave Jesus a number of answers. Then Jesus said, "But who do you say that I am?" (Matt. 16:15).

Jesus is still going around asking the same question. I have answered that question for myself. My hope is that this book will help you find an answer for yourself. Anyway, after you read what follows, you won't be able to say, "Nobody ever told me."

2 A HERITAGE OF CHARACTER

If Jesus has come...
what is He like?

And the Word became flesh, and dwelt among us, and we beheld his glory as of the only begotten from the Father, full of grace and truth.

John 1:14

Someone has said that today's young people don't have any trouble with Jesus, but they don't like the church. I can understand having trouble with the church (occasionally, I have my problems with the church, too), but what I can't understand is why someone would not have trouble with Jesus. I love Jesus, but it would be dishonest for me to say that I have not had and still never have any trouble with Him.

My associate, Dave O'Dowd, was recently on a radio talk show debating with another man on the subject of capital punishment. Dave's position was that capital punishment, when carried out with justice, is not just permitted in the Bible, but is commanded in the Bible. Dave is a very good polemicist, and he clearly was winning the debate. The man with whom he was debating had one final argument, however, and he thought that with it he would win the day. He said to Dave, "Let me ask you a question. Do you believe that if a man were tried and convicted, Jesus Christ would pull the lever on the electric chair?"

Dave's answer was classic. He said to the gentleman, "Sir, it is clear that you not only are cursed with an inadequate knowledge of the Bible; it is clear that you don't know much about

Jesus either. Not only would He pull the lever, but the Bible says that He is going to do a lot more than that."

Dave had pointed out one of the great misconceptions about Jesus, namely, that Jesus is merely gentle, meek, and mild. Most people who deny Jesus Christ actually have never rejected Him in the sense that they have never encountered the real Jesus. Surprisingly enough, many of those who claim the name of Jesus have never encountered His reality either.

For a while, let's talk about the real Jesus—not the one you think you know, but the real, genuine article. You may be surprised about Him when you meet Him. In this discussion we will, I would remind you, be talking about Jesus to His face. In other words, as I write this and as you read it, Jesus, the Watcher, is present. It is a good thing to keep in mind.

When I first met my wife, Anna, I didn't know a thing about her. I didn't know the name of her hometown; I had never met her parents, and I didn't even know their names. I didn't know if she had any brothers or sisters, or whether she liked spinach. I didn't know her political or religious views. But I did know a few things about her: she was beautiful, articulate, and winsome. I found out about the other things later, after I knew her.

I suspect that most of the people we meet are like that. We know them before we know about them. Let's meet Jesus that way. Let's imagine meeting this Person for the first time.

A Great Concern for God

The first thing you would note upon meeting Jesus would be His great concern for God. You wouldn't be around Him very long before you would hear references to His Father.

I have often maintained that the best thing to do with new Christians is to lock them up for about a year. Their enthusiasm is wonderful, but they have not discovered the balance that comes with maturity. A new Christian has discovered something so wonderful and meaningful that he or she wants to share it with everyone whether or not that sharing is appropriate in a given situation.

One of the reasons Paul required that a leader of the church not be a new convert (see 1 Tim. 3:6) is that he understood the balance that comes with time. Sometimes when you are around a new Christian, you get the feeling he is trying to twist every conversation, every reference, every observation around to the point of talking about God.

A man came to me one time with a complaint about his Christian wife. He said, "Reverend, I'm interested in the Christian faith, but if you don't call off my wife, I'll never become a Christian. I can't talk with her anymore without talking about religion: I can't sit down to read the paper without having a tract fall out; I can't even go into the bathroom without finding a Bible open and some verses underlined. I am fast becoming an atheist because of my wife." I understood his problem. New Christians have a tendency to force others to consider Christ.

But a mature Christian is different. If a Christian has grown properly, he or she will make many references to God, but the references will be natural. There will be no need to manipulate the conversation around to religious matters; religious matters will be a natural part of conversation.

If you are around me very long, you will hear me mention my wife and my children. I don't look for opportunities to talk about them; I don't have to remember to bring them up in conversation. They are such a natural part of my life, such an integral part of the person I am, that you can't know me very long without knowing something about my family. A mature Christian's references to God are sort of like that.

The best example of this kind of maturity is found in Jesus Christ. A good illustration of His concern for God is found in the fourth chapter of the gospel of John. Jesus was waiting for His disciples by a well in Sychar in Samaria. He was thirsty and tired, and a woman of Samaria came to the well to draw water. Jesus asked her for a drink. In very quick order the conversation turned to spiritual things, and eventually to the woman's recognition of Jesus as a man of God. The whole incident is recounted with revealing commentary from John:

And from that city many of the Samaritans believed in Him because of the word of the woman who testified, "He told me all the things that I have done." So when the Samaritans came to Him, they were asking Him to stay with them; and He stayed there two days. And many more believed because of His word; and they were saying to the woman, "It is no longer because of what you said that we believe, for we have heard for ourselves and know that this One is indeed the Savior of the world." (John 4:39–42)

Jesus was not forced, or manipulative, or phony. Jesus had a great concern for God, and if you were to spend time with Jesus today, it wouldn't be long before you recognized you were talking to someone who knew God by more than hearsay.

I have a friend who is a new pilot. He has just received his pilot's license after hours of work and practice. He is so caught up in his new hobby that he talks about it all the time. My friend is so enthusiastic about flying that I even find myself sharing his enthusiasm. (You need to know that although I do a lot of flying, it is not one of my favorite things to do. I rate it right under jumping off buildings. I have yet to put all my weight on an airplane.) Jesus' love for God was so great that those who were around Him found themselves caught up in that same love.

One time an American was visiting the Metropolitan Tabernacle in London when Charles Spurgeon was the pastor. After the service, an Englishman asked the American, "Well, what did you think of him?"

The American replied, "What did I think of whom?"

"Why," said the Englishman, "Spurgeon, of course."

"To be perfectly honest with you," said the American, "I was not thinking about Spurgeon at all. I was thinking about Christ."

It's hard to think about Jesus without thinking about God the Father, because He was His major concern. It was by Him that Christ defined Himself. He prayed, "O righteous Father, although the world has not known Thee, yet I have known Thee; and these have known that Thou didst send Me; and I have made Thy name known to them" (John 17:25–26a).

Just as it is difficult to think of Romeo without thinking of Juliet, or of Cupid without thinking of Psyche, or of Simon without thinking of Garfunkel, so it is difficult to think of Jesus without thinking of God. If you should meet Him for the first time, you would notice that fact. He has a great concern for God.

A Great Concern for Truth

But, also, if you should meet Jesus for the first time, you would be impressed with His great concern for the truth. Someone said that people are driven either by fear or by truth. I wouldn't say that Jesus was "driven" by truth, but He had a central concern about truth. John said about Jesus, "And the Word became flesh, and dwelt among us, and we beheld His glory, glory as of the only begotten from the Father, full of grace and truth" (John 1:14). When Jesus spoke of Himself, He said, "I am the...truth" (John 14:6). When Jesus stood before Pilate for judgment, one gets the feeling that it was not Jesus who was being judged. In response to Pilate's comment that Jesus was perhaps a king, He said, "You say correctly that I am a king. For this I have been born, and for this I have come into the world, to bear witness to the truth. Every one who is of the truth hears my voice" (John 18:37).

Have you ever met a person who was more concerned about honesty than about being liked? I have a daughter like that, and she has the ability to make you feel uncomfortable if you would rather have people say nice things than tell the truth. My daughter Robin simply is incapable of hiding the truth. In fact, because I am a pastor and public relations is rather important, I have always thought that Robin could have been a little less interested in telling people the truth. Now, I don't mean that I want her to lie; I just would rather she not say everything she thinks.

When Robin was to be interviewed by the admissions people at the college she had chosen to attend, she was very worried that she would not be accepted. It was a difficult college to get into because of its high academic standards. Because it was a

Christian school, the admissions people would be impressed by a number of things, and dress was one of them. Thus, her mother was rather shocked when she noticed that Robin dressed for the interview in blue jeans. Anna said to Robin, "Don't you think it would be wise to wear a dress?"

Robin answered, "Mom, I really want to be accepted, but I don't want to be accepted because I wear a dress. I want to be accepted just the way I am." As a matter of fact, she was accepted, and maybe it was because she wore jeans.

The point is this: Robin is interested in the truth, in telling it and living it, and she is interested in the truth because she is very close to Jesus. It rubs off, you know.

If you should meet Jesus for the first time, you would feel a bit uncomfortable. He wouldn't say nice things to you just to make you feel good. He would tell you the truth. At first you would want to go to someone else. But after a while you would realize how precious the truth really is, and you would find yourself being drawn to Him. Later you would learn to trust Him because He would never tell you a lie.

There is an interesting incident in the sixth chapter of John with which I can identify. The crowds had been following Jesus the way one would follow a magician or a motivational speaker. They wanted Him to do some more magic tricks or to tell them something that would make them healthy, wealthy, and wise. And then Jesus started teaching hard lessons about commitment. The crowds started leaving and the followers of Jesus started getting down to the muscle. The crowds were thinking, *We didn't sign up for this*. After a great number of people had left, Jesus turned to His disciples and said, "What about you guys? Are you going to leave, too?"

Peter spoke for the rest of the disciples (and for a lot of others who have found the truth in Jesus), "Lord, to whom shall we go? You have words of eternal life. And we have believed and have come to know that You are the Holy One of God" (John 6:68–69). You see, truth is addicting. Once you start dealing with the truth, you just can't settle for a lie.

If you are tired of the con men and the hucksters, then you would like Jesus. His truth is sometimes hard truth; sometimes you won't like His truth. There will even be times when you will wish you had never heard His truth. But it is truth, and truth is a precious and rare commodity in our world.

I recently went to get my car fixed. I don't know much about automobiles, but I do know when they don't work, and mine wasn't working. The mechanic examined the engine and told me that I needed a part he didn't have in stock. He said, "Mr. Brown, I will order the part and call you in two or three days."

"Look," I said, "I don't care if it takes three weeks to get the part, but don't lie to me and tell me that the part will be here in three days when it won't be here for three weeks. I understand the problems, and I understand that it is sometimes difficult to get a part, but if you want me to be your customer, don't ever lie to me."

He smiled and said, "Well, Mr. Brown, to be perfectly honest with you, it might take a week or even ten days to get the part."

I don't know about you, but I'm tired of having to tell people to tell me the truth. Jesus will never say to you, "To be perfectly honest with you..." He is always honest, and you can assume so when you go to Him. If you would rather be given information that is easy to swallow, if you would rather hear things that will make you feel comfortable, if you would rather hear the slick line of the world's peddlers of trinkets, you won't care much for Jesus because Jesus has an overwhelming concern for truth.

A Great Concern for People

Finally, you need to know that if you go to Jesus, you will note that He not only has a great concern for God and for truth, but He also has a great concern for people in general and for you in particular. The Scripture says that the people followed Jesus gladly. They still do, and do you know why? Because He cares—He really cares.

When Jesus called two fishermen named Andrew and Peter, He knew they were looking for meaning for their lives, and He made them fishers of men. When He called Nathanael, He pointed out Nathanael's gentleness and vulnerability. He had time to stoop low to listen to a child whisper in His ear, and He didn't turn away from lepers. He reached out to the rich and the poor, the famous and the infamous, the powerful and the weak. He was concerned about a father who had lost a child and about a man who was losing his faith. He was kind to those for whom society had no kindness; He was forgiving toward those for whom religious people had no forgiveness; He was loving toward the unlovely. And with all He had to do, He cared enough about a friend who was having a wedding party to make sure His friend had enough wine for his guests.

You could have asked almost anyone who encountered Jesus—the lepers who had been made clean, the blind people who had been given their sight, the cripples who had thrown away their crutches. They all would have told you Jesus cared.

Hundreds of years before the birth of Christ, Isaiah predicted the coming of the Messiah. One of the interesting things about his prediction is that Isaiah pictured more than just a figure of great power and authority—he pictured a Servant. The servant passages in Isaiah are fascinating, because with each passage Isaiah allows us to see something more about the Servant-Messiah. And then in the fifty-third chapter of Isaiah, the prophet takes our breath away with a description of a suffering, caring, dying Servant.

> But He was pierced through
>   for our transgressions,
> He was crushed for our iniquities;
> The chastening for our well-being
>   fell upon Him.
> And by His scourging we are healed.
> All of us like sheep have gone astray,
> Each of us has turned to his own way;
> But the Lord has caused the iniquity
>   of us all to fall on Him.
> He was oppressed and He was afflicted,
> Yet He did not open His mouth;
> Like a lamb that is led to slaughter,
> And like a sheep that is silent
>   before its shearers,
> So He did not open His mouth. (vv. 5–7)

The thirteenth chapter of John is one of the best places to see this essential nature of Jesus as a Servant. You will remember that Jesus was at the Last Supper with His disciples. We know from the synoptic gospels that He had been talking about the fact that if a person wants to be great he has to be a servant. Jesus, knowing that the disciples had not understood His teaching, took a towel and a basin of water and began to wash the disciples' feet. Peter probably expressed the feelings of everyone around the table when he refused to allow Jesus to wash his feet. In response to Peter's protest, Jesus said, "If I do not wash you, you have no part of Me" (v. 8). In other words, Jesus was saying that in order to understand what His Messiahship is all about, one must allow the Messiah to serve. Jesus said, "The Son of Man did not come to be served, but to serve, and to give His life a ransom for many" (Matt. 20:28).

What do you think was bothering Peter when Jesus began to wash Peter's feet? Let me tell you: he simply couldn't understand the role reversal. If Jesus had commanded Peter to wash Jesus' feet, Peter would have known how to respond because leaders are supposed to command and servants are supposed to serve masters. But Jesus became the servant; the Master washed the servant's feet; Jesus reversed the roles.

If you go to Jesus, you will be surprised the way Peter was surprised. You probably will be embarrassed and shocked because Jesus will serve you, too. He cares, and someone who cares always serves the object he cares for. You will find that He cares. He really cares.

You see, being concerned about God isn't enough. There are lots of folks who have a concern for God but don't care very much at all about people. I have a friend who is with Youth for Christ, and he says that he sometimes tells God, "Father, I could get this job done if it weren't for all these kids." He says that God always answers, "Son, those kids *are* your job." Sometimes it is possible to be concerned about God and forget about the world for which He gave His Son.

That is why God seems so distant sometimes to those who know the most about Him. Saint Teresa said she was praying once when she had a magnificent vision of God. She said she was actually in His presence. In the midst of the vision, there was a knock at the door, and she wavered between staying on her knees and going to the door to help whoever it was who knocked. Finally, she left her prayers to go to the door. When she returned, Jesus was still there. She said, "I was afraid that you would be gone."

He replied, "My child, if you had not gone to the door, I would not have remained."

The best way to tell whether a person has been with God is to see what that person thinks about people. Jesus cared deeply for people. That is what the cross was all about. He cared enough about them to do more than tell them about God and tell them the truth. He cared enough about them to die on a cross, accepting the punishment they deserved.

One time the Skinner Sprinkler Systems Company got on the computerized mailing list of a magazine publisher as S. Sprinkler. There was considerable merriment around the office of the sprinkler company when they received a letter that read, "Dear Mr. Sprinkler, only your name is important to us. Because to us you are more than a name, you are valuable to us. You are not just a number; you are S. Sprinkler, a unique individual, a person we would like to be friends with."

Do you ever get the feeling that you are on the world's computerized mailing list and that nobody knows your name or cares whether you live or die? I do sometimes, and then I think of Jesus. His caring is real, and it is individualized. That is a rare and precious commodity in our world.

I have a friend in Dallas who spends a great part of his life on the speaker's circuit. The thing I like about this friend is that he doesn't allow his speeches to get in the way of people. Sometimes he will pick out someone in the crowd, more often than not a loser, and he will spend some time with that person, fanning the flame of his or her potential.

Recently he received a call from a woman who attended Baylor University years before and had heard him speak there. He had taken a personal interest in this young woman but he had not heard from her in the years that followed. She asked on the phone, "Do you remember me?"

He not only told her that he remembered her, but he told her a number of specific things he remembered about her. She was overwhelmed that he still remembered.

And then the woman said to him, "I have had a very difficult life since those years at Baylor. I have been through a divorce, a major illness, and a considerable amount of tragedy. And do you know what kept me going all these years? I kept going because I remembered that a fat man in Dallas believed in me."

Jesus is like this friend, at least in one particular way. He will take someone who doesn't have any hope left and introduce him to the Father. Then He will tell him the truth about himself—not necessarily pleasant truth, but necessary truth. Then He will love that person enough to cause that person to believe and to hope. That's what He did for Simon. He gave him a nickname. He called him "the rock." Everyone else, I suppose, laughed. But Jesus believed in Peter's potential, and Peter became what Jesus expected. He became the rock. Jesus does that. He goes around believing in people, not because people are so wonderful, but because His grace and love are so great.

Things haven't always been wonderful in my life. When I finally found the Watcher and discovered that He was Jesus, my life changed—but all the problems, the hurt, and the failure didn't go away. There have been times when I wanted to give up and just run away. But I haven't. I'm still following and changing and growing. Do you know why? Because a strange man on a cross believes in me. That has made all the difference in the world.

You will discover that difference, too, if you ever really meet Him.

3 A HERITAGE OF TRUTH

If Jesus has come...
I've heard from God.

God, after He spoke long ago to the fathers in the prophets in many ways, in these last days has spoken to us in His Son.

Hebrews 1:1–2a

Recently, I have been going through some rather radical changes in my life. When I became a Christian, the act was almost totally an intellectual decision. I searched for truth; I found truth; I acted accordingly. The Christian faith has not been for me, until recently, anything that had much to do with my heart as much as it had to do with my head. I was faithful to Christ, not because it made me feel good or because I "felt" close to God, but because I had decided that the Christian faith was true.

Now you must understand that there is nothing wrong with being faithful to Christ because you are acting according to the truth you know. As a matter of fact, I have noted after talking to a lot of Christians that most Christians could use a little more fact and a little less feeling. Sometimes it is hard to separate experiential Christianity from an overactive endocrine gland. In a marriage, the expression says, "Kissin' don't last but cookin' do." Just so, in a genuine walk with God, feeling sometimes doesn't last when the truth does.

However, with all of that said, more needs to be said. After a number of years of following the truth simply because it is true, I came to the realization that the Christian faith must be more than just facts. I would listen to the testimonies of my brothers and sisters in Christ. They would talk about how Christ was real to them and of how they had experienced His presence in some very clear and deep ways. When I listened to them talk, I knew that something was missing in my life. I knew a lot about God; I had read hundreds of books about Him. I was a Bible teacher and I knew the Bible and loved its great truths. But something was still missing. Sure, there had been those rare occasions when I had experienced God in a significant way. There had been those times when my prayer life had reality to it, and there had been those times when I was stirred emotionally. However, those experiences were few and far between. Most of the time, God seemed to have gone away on vacation somewhere in Bermuda and left me with a whole lot to do.

I had gone too far to get out, so leaving Him was simply not an option. I remember a Methodist minister friend of mine who, after we had spent many hours together discussing the veracity of the Bible, decided he was going to do something about the truth he had discovered. He decided to have a series of evangelistic services in his church. He invited a well-known evangelist and advertised throughout the city. He was excited about what was going to happen.

I talked to him the next morning after the first service and asked him how it had gone. He said, "Steve, not one person came...not one. The speaker and I just went out to dinner together."

Later my friend had a series of bad physical experiences that seemed like heart attacks. Each time he was taken to the emergency room of the hospital and was told the doctors could not find anything physically wrong with him. He stopped by my study one day, and as soon as the door was closed he started to weep. He said, "I wish I could get out of this. I wish I had never learned the truths of God, but I have gone too far and see too much to get out."

I understood my friend's problem. In fact, it was my problem, too, so I went to the Father and prayed, "God, You know that I have gone too far to get out, and so this isn't a threat. If

You answer this prayer in the positive or negative, I will still be Your man. I will still teach Your Word, and I will still follow Your ways. But Father, I'm tired of just knowing about You, talking about You, and teaching about You. I want to know You, and I want to pay whatever price it costs to know You. Father, I'm so tired of hearsay. Come and reveal Yourself to me. That will be enough."

I would like to tell you that right after that prayer I heard a voice from heaven, saw a vision, or experienced a powerful manifestation of God's Spirit. I would like to say that I had a second working of grace, or that I was given a great spiritual gift. I would like to say that, but I can't say it because it didn't happen.

Let me tell you what did happen. God began to work in a subtle process in my life. I began taking more time just to be quiet before the Father. I started reading less theology and reading more of the great devotional masters of the Church. I stopped, as much as possible, what a friend of mine calls "blithering" before God. I started listening and worshiping and adoring. And slowly I have found the Father answering my prayer for Himself. As I have learned to "work from the silence" of His presence, maybe for the first time in my life I have been able to say on occasion, "This morning I was with the Father." I have found the Bible more alive than ever before, and theology is not just a system of doctrine. It has become the description of the One I know and love.

It is one thing to know the truth about someone, and it is quite another to know the person to whom the truth refers. In other words, you can know everything about a person, but it isn't the same thing as knowing the person.

I love the story of Simeon. You will find his story in the second chapter of the gospel according to Luke. He served in the temple in Jerusalem in the first century. He was a godly man who had been told by the Lord that he would see the Messiah before he died. Now you need to know that Simeon knew the truth about God, and he understood the prophecy about the coming Messiah. He had walked in God's ways all his life, and he was familiar with God's Word. But Simeon was promised he'd see for himself.

When Mary and Joseph brought Jesus to the temple for circumcision, Simeon took their little baby in his arms, and he knew that God had fulfilled His promise. God had allowed all his hopes to become reality. Simeon's song is one of the most beautiful in the Bible: "Now Lord, Thou dost let Thy bondservant depart in peace, according to Thy Word; for my eyes have seen Thy salvation, which Thou hast prepared in the presence of all peoples. A light of revelation to the Gentiles, and the glory of Thy people Israel" (Luke 2:29–32). In other words, Simeon said, "Lord, I have seen the reality, and now I can go home."

Simeon knew the truth about God; he knew the Scriptures; he knew prophecy. But finally he knew God's Son; he had touched the reality. I can understand Simeon because I asked for the same thing from God. I knew the truth about God, but I wanted to know Him myself. That hope is becoming a reality in my life. Is it changing my theology? No. Is it causing me to think differently about God? No. Have I been surprised? No. But to know the One I have worshiped and followed for so long is a whole lot better than simply knowing about Him.

God's Self-Revelation

I have said all of the above to introduce the most important and exciting fact of history: the incarnation of God in Christ. The Scripture says, "God was in Christ reconciling the world to Himself " (2 Cor. 5:19). That means that God has come and revealed Himself with Himself. He has not just used words, He has used action. He has entered time and space, and the reality is wondrous to behold.

For thousands of years, mortals looked into the heavens and wondered. Is there a God, and if there is a God, what is He like? Is He a monster demanding the sacrifice of my children? Is He a God who started the machinery and then left it alone? Is He a God of love and compassion, or is He a God who has turned His back? Does He care? And then the important question, "does He care about *me*?"

There were, of course, those who spoke the truth. You can read their words in the Bible, and they were right about Him. Abraham made a covenant with God and told others about it. Moses said that God was the great "I am," and he was right. Joshua convinced the people of God that God would make them victorious in battle, and he was right. David wrote poetry about God, and the poetry was more than words; the poetry was truth. The prophets spoke about the God who commands and judges and loves. They were right, too. Oh yes, a lot of people knew about God, and, believe it or not, their information was accurate. The problem was that information is never enough to satisfy fully.

And then God, the God about whom so many had spoken, spoke. His laughter spilled over into a world that had forgotten how to laugh—except the laughter of derision and cynicism. God entered time and space, and the world would never be the same.

"In the beginning was the Word." (Lots of folks knew that.) "And the Word was with God." (Interesting and true theology.) *"And the Word became flesh and dwelt among us"* (emphasis added). Now that is different! The hope became a reality; the words took on meaning; the bones took on flesh; God became a man. God spoke, and for the first time people didn't have to ask questions and wonder. It was there for everyone to see. The Word of God had become flesh.

Now think about that! The God who created the world, who sustains the world and who continues the world for His reasons—that God has come. The omnipotent, omnipresent, omniscient God has come to a finite world. He has become vulnerable to His creation. He has become man.

I have a friend who was at a party where a professor of theology had gotten a little tipsy. The professor leaned over to my friend and said, "You know, I really don't believe all the things I teach are true."

My friend, a theological scholar whose intellect has not

blinded him to the truth, smiled and answered, "Yes, I know you don't believe it's true. But don't you wish it were?" The inebriated theologian, my friend said, looked as if he were going to weep.

I believe a great deal of the disbelief of our time regarding Christianity has as much to do with a fear of disappointment as with intellectual questions. That was Thomas's problem. You will remember that Jesus had appeared to the disciples after His death. To understate the situation, they were excited about the fact that a dead man had gotten out of His grave, and the first person they told was Thomas. Thomas sounded like a wet, shaggy dog shaking himself at a Miss America Pageant. He said, "Unless I shall see in His hands the imprint of the nails, and put my finger into the place of the nails, and put my hand into His side, I will not believe" (John 20:25). I can understand Thomas. He had been devastated by the death of the One he loved. He was just getting used to the idea of His death, and someone was trying to stir up hope.

I was sitting next to a woman on a plane the other day when the subject of Christianity came up. When she learned that I was a pastor, it was clear the conversation had come to an end. She said to me, "Look Reverend, I don't want to hear what you have to say. I have been disappointed too much already. I simply can't afford to invest in hope again."

In *Pilgrim's Progress*, you will remember, Mercy had laughed in her sleep. Christina asked her the reason for her laughter, and Mercy answered:

> I dreamed that I sat alone in a solitary place, and was bemoaning of the hardness of my heart. Now I had not sat there long, but methought many were gathered about to see me, and to hear what it was that I said.... Some of them laughed at me, some called me fool, and some began to thrust me about. With that, methought I looked up and saw one coming with wings toward me. So he came directly to me, and said "Mercy, what aileth thee?" Now when he had heard me make my complaint, he said, "Peace be to thee"; he also wiped mine eyes with his handkerchief, and clad me in silver and gold. He put a chain about my neck, and ear-rings in my ears, and a beautiful crown upon my head. Then he took me by

the hand, and said, "Mercy, come after me." So he went up, and I followed till we came at a golden gate... and I followed him up to a throne, upon which One sat; and He said to me, "Welcome, daughter." The place looked bright and twinkling, like the stars, or rather like the sun, and I thought that I saw your husband there; so I awoke from my dream. But did I laugh?

What a wonderful dream, and the most wonderful thing about Mercy's dream was that it was not a dream, it was reality. We forget our dreams. Some we forget because they are so horrible, and others we forget because they are so beautiful. On the one hand we can't stand the horror, and on the other we can't stand the hope.

The good news about the incarnation is that the dream has come true. The hopes of millions have been confirmed. Reality has entered a world where men and women were afraid to hope too much lest they be disappointed too much. Beyond our wildest dreams, God has turned the fairy tale into reality. There is meaning, there is joy, there is forgiveness, there is hope, there is freedom. There is a happy ending. God has spoken! The Word has become flesh!

World History's Preparation for Jesus

If you will, allow me to give you a short history lesson. There are two great streams of human history. One is the Judeo-Christian stream of human history. Some two thousand years before the birth of Christ, a group of nobodies in the middle of the desert came up with the crazy idea that God had chosen them to be His people. These nobodies lived in the midst of cultures far more sophisticated and civilized than their own. One would have expected that these Hebrews (many believe that the word *Hebrew* comes from a word meaning "wanderer" or "nomad") would have been absorbed into cultures that surrounded them. That is the way things happen in the "real" world. But in this case it didn't happen. In fact, just the opposite happened.

Living among people who sacrificed their children to their gods, people who worshiped the sun and the moon, people who made idols and worshiped the creation of their hands, these Hebrews developed the highest form of monotheism the world had ever known. Their ethical and moral value system was incredibly sophisticated, and their theology was far ahead of anything yet seen on the face of the earth.

One of the great mysteries of history is the Hebrew religion. From a sociological standpoint, there is simply no explanation for its development and perseverance. From a biblical standpoint, there is no mystery at all. They really were God's people, they had been chosen, they were right. Be that as it may, this stream of human history began to move down a corridor of time.

Now let's turn to the Greco-Roman stream of human history. It started in the twelfth century B.C. with the Greek conquest of the Aegean civilization, and it moved through the Athenian golden age, the Peloponnesian War, the conquest and rule of Alexander the Great, and finally to the rule of Rome. Within this stream of human history we find our political roots. Here we find great learning, philosophy, architecture, art, and science. When the Romans ruled, there was a common language, a common coinage, a common road system, and, best of all, peace (that is, the *Pax Romana*).

These two great streams of history moved in parallel and separate corridors of history for more than a thousand years. Now here is the interesting thing about this lesson in human history. *In the first century, these two streams of human history crossed.* And do you know what happened when they crossed? Let me tell you: a Jew by the name of Jesus was born in a stable in Bethlehem. If Jesus had been born seventy years earlier (given the Parthians' occupation of Jerusalem), you would never have heard His name. If Jesus has been born seventy years later (given the fall of Jerusalem), you would never have known His story. For the first time in human history, it was possible for a story to spread throughout the Western world. For the first time in human history, an idea could be heard by men and women everywhere. For the first time in human history, it was possible for a man born in a little village in a small country, never traveling more than forty miles from His hometown, to be known and loved by thousands in countries and cultures far different from His own.

Now consider, if you will, the above data. Do you think it was an accident? Do you think it was just one of those coincidences that happen occasionally in the annals of history? Or do you think that maybe, just maybe, God planned it all? Do you think that maybe, just maybe, all of history was prepared for this one event? Could it be, do you think, that God prepared the conditions under which His coming would be the most favorable? The Bible says that like the great communicator He is, God waited until the audience became quiet before He spoke.

World Culture's Preparation for Jesus

One of the great passages in the Bible is the first eighteen verses of the gospel of John. In these verses are words and concepts that, when you understand the context, boggle your mind. You will note that the passage begins with the words "In the beginning was the Word." You will find these same words in the first book of the Bible. In Genesis 1:1, the Bible opens this way: "In the beginning God..."

I believe that John (and he is a good friend of mine) was thinking about the first beginning in Genesis when he wrote the first part of his gospel. (In passing, you ought to note that John uses words in his opening remarks that are important in Genesis 1. He talks about "life" [John 1:4], about "light" [John 1:4], and about "darkness" [John 1:5].)

The apostle John was looking back to Genesis 1:1, and inspired by the Holy Spirit, he spoke of another beginning—a beginning just as important, wonderful, and fantastic as the first beginning. In both accounts the darkness, chaos, and confusion were interrupted by light, clarity, and consistency. In the first beginning God began time, and in the second He made the hours count; in the first beginning God created the process, and in the second God gave the process meaning; in the first beginning God instituted His plan, and in the second God unveiled the plan to humankind.

I remember when our baby daughters were brought home from the hospital. I recall how I felt on each occasion as I examined their tiny hands, their fragile bodies, and their beginning efforts at life. What a wondrous thing God had done! What a great gift! What a joyous occasion! John must have felt that same way as he looked at the universe and examined its beginnings. At first he saw God's beginning creation, and then he saw God's beginning surprise.

Now let me show you something very important. In the Bible, words are not just a combination of letters and sounds to translate ideas. They don't just express ideas or realities. In the Bible, words *are* a reality. We say, "Sticks and stones may break my bones, but words can never hurt me." In the Bible that is simply not true. Let me illustrate. In Genesis 26, Jacob stole Esau's birthright by tricking Isaac into giving him a blessing. We say, "Big deal! What possible difference could that make? A blessing is just words, right?" Wrong. The importance of words, in the biblical sense, is that they have a reality all their own. Once the blessing was uttered by Isaac, it could not be retracted. Jacob's receiving the blessing was a final reality.

At the end of most worship services there is a place for a benediction. Have you ever thought about that? A benediction is a blessing, and it is not meaningless. It is the pronouncing of words with power of blessing on a congregation. The Bible, incidentally, has a number of maledictions that are taken very seriously as well, and they are taken seriously because words have their own reality. Words have power.

Let me give you a principle and then some Scripture verses. The principle is this: words have power in direct proportion to the reality and the ultimate power of the one speaking the words. Listen to how *words* or *word* is expressed in the Bible: "By the word of the Lord the heavens were made" (Ps. 33:6); "He sent His word and healed them, and delivered them from their destructions" (Ps. 107:20); "He sends forth his command to the earth; His word runs very swiftly" (Ps. 147:15); "So shall

My word be which goes forth from My mouth; it shall not return to Me empty, without accomplishing what I desire, and without succeeding in the matter for which I sent it" (Isa. 55:11).

Along with this, in the Wisdom Literature of the Old Testament, and later during the period between the Testaments, the "wisdom of God" became an important concept. Wisdom was personified as in Proverbs 3:13–19: "How blessed is the man who finds wisdom.... *She* is more precious than jewels.... Long life is in *her* right hand; in *her* left hand are riches and honor.... The Lord by wisdom founded the earth." Wisdom, with the alternative and developing meaning of *reason* and *word*, is an important concept in the Old Testament.

If you will, I want to put all of that on the back burner for just a moment as we turn to the Greek development of a similar concept. As early as 560 B.C. in Ephesus, Greek philosophy was beginning to take shape. The philosopher Heraclitus said the earth was changing all the time: the reason you can't go home again is that home is constantly changing, and the reason you can't step into the same river twice is that the river is constantly changing. This state of flux described by the Greeks has to be held together by something. Do you know what they said held things together? The *logos* or the "word" of God (though their definition of it was not the same as that of the Jews). Stoics got a piece of the philosophical action, too. They said that order is brought out of chaos by (you guessed it) the word. In Alexandria, a great Jew by the name of Philo saw what was happening in both cultures and brought the whole idea together.

All right, you ask, so what? I'll tell you so what: note that throughout the centuries both the Jews and the Greeks were developing a concept independently of one another by which both could understand the incarnation of Christ. Do you see it? God not only prepared history, but He also prepared the cultural thought forms of different civilizations to understand the coming of Christ. When John wrote, "In the beginning was the Word, and the Word was with God, and the Word was God.... And the Word became flesh," he was speaking a message that could be understood by everyone. The word *logos* he used for "the word" was not just Jewish or Greek or Roman. It was universal.

Do you think it was just an accident? Do you think that it was just one of those interesting side roads of linguistics? Or, do you think that maybe, just maybe, God planned it all? The Bible teaches that before God spoke, He made sure that He would be understood. Someone has said, "Before you criticize what I say, you should demonstrate that you understand what I said." God made sure that the world would understand before He spoke.

World Religious Preparation for Jesus

Stay with me for just a little longer, and I will show you something else of great interest. From earliest recorded history, we know that there has been a universal acceptance of the concept of sacrifice. All cultures about which we have information have believed that "without shedding of blood there is no forgiveness" (Heb. 9:22). The ideas were primitive and unsophisticated, but the concept was the same: sacrifice was necessary in the economy of gods or God.

The concept of sacrifice was wide and undefined until the Jews came along and gave it new meaning. In the biblical account of the Passover (see Exod. 12), an exciting idea begins to develop. You will remember that God freed His people from Egypt (after a number of false starts from Pharaoh) by causing the death of the first-born throughout the land. God, however, allowed the Jews to escape this terrible tragedy. How? They were to sacrifice a lamb, and the blood of the lamb was to be placed on the doorposts and lintels of their houses.

Throughout the history of the Jews, the idea of sacrifice developed and was defined. Sacrifice was for the sins of the people. However, note that all the sacrifices of all the Jews, and all the sacrifices of all people from all time, could not take away one sin. The writer of Hebrews said this: "For it is impossible for the blood of bulls and goats to take away sins" (10:4).

Put that on the back burner for just a moment while I show you something of Greek thinking. Plato developed a system of thought more than three centuries before the birth of Christ that said the world of ordinary experience is illusory and the real world is the world of ideas or forms. Everything we see and experience is only a shadow of the real.

Plato illustrated this idea with what has been called the "parable of the cave." In this parable, as recounted in the *Republic*, he imagined people living in a cave underground with an entrance open to the light. These people had lived since birth chained to the wall of the cave. All they could see was shadows on the cave wall of those who lived outside the cave, and the people never saw what was making the shadows. Plato suggested that these chained people would believe to be real that which was only a shadow. He said that which we think of as real is only a shadow like that on the wall of the cave. The real is the idea or the form.

This is not the place for a discussion of whether Plato is right. But—and here is the important point for our discussion—his thoughts became an easy method to communicate the idea of incarnation and sacrifice. Let me show you. Hebrews 10:1 says, "For the Law, since it has only a shadow of the good things to come and not the very form of things, can never by the same sacrifices year by year...make perfect those who draw near." The writer then went on to show that Christ was real, whereas the other sacrifices were shadows. He wrote, "And every priest stands daily ministering and offering time after time the same sacrifices, which can never take away sins; but He, having offered one sacrifice for sins for all time, sat down at the right hand of God" (vv. 11–12).

Do you see it? God, from the beginning of recorded history, was preparing the world to understand and accept the implications of the incarnation. When John the Baptist called Jesus the "Lamb of God" (see John 1:36), he was pointing to the culmination of thousands of years of preparation, articulated by the Jews and revealed in Jesus. Peter wrote this: "You were not redeemed with perishable things like silver or gold from your futile way of life inherited from your forefathers, but with precious blood, as of a lamb unblemished and spotless, the blood of Christ" (1 Pet. 1:18–19). Peter's words carried the meaning of God's preparation thousands of years before he wrote them. God had planted the idea of sacrifice so that when He spoke the world would understand. Not only that, but He also had enabled the concept of shadow and reality to explain the incarnation.

Do you think it was an accident? Do you think it was merely a coincidence? Do you think it was a game with words and ideas? If you think so, I have some swampland to sell you in Florida!

So what is it that I have been saying? I have been saying that God has come. History points to it; cultural thought-forms testify to its reality; even pagan religions anticipated part of it; and a loving, guiding, and sovereign hand prepared for it. God has spoken in Christ. He has come so that we wouldn't only have to know *about* Him. He has come that we might know *Him*.

Every Christmas Paul Harvey tells the story about a man who was an atheist. His wife and children did not share his unbelief, and every Christmas Eve they went to the Christmas Eve service at the church while the man stayed at home and read the paper. When the family returned from the service, they opened their presents and celebrated the holiday. The atheist was not a bad man. He just was not a hypocrite, and he couldn't buy all of the nonsense about God's becoming a man.

On one particular Christmas Eve, the family had gone to church and the man was reading the paper. He heard a noise coming from the living room window, and he went to check. He found that a snowstorm had developed and that the birds outside, trying to escape the storm, were trying to get into the house by flying against the picture window. They saw the warmth of the house through the window, and they were flying against it and falling to the ground.

With the compassion that we sometimes feel for hurt creatures, the man decided to do something about the birds. He put on his heavy coat and boots and went out to the yard. He tried to shoo the birds away from the window, but to the birds he was an enemy and they flew away from him, against the window. The man walked down to the barn, opened the doors, and turned on the light, thinking that the birds would see the light and fly into the barn for its warmth. But as he tried to get them to see, they only flew from him, frightened by his efforts to help.

As he stood in the storm and watched the birds, the man thought to himself, *Those dumb birds. They simply don't understand. If I could just find a way to communicate with them. If I could just find a way to let them know that I am not their enemy. If*—if I could only become a bird, *I would make them understand.*

At that moment the bells on the church steeple began to ring, signaling the end of the Christmas Eve service. As the man heard the bells, he thought of God, whose feelings were not dissimilar to his own in trying to communicate with the birds. In a flash of understanding and insight, the man realized what Christmas was about, and he fell on his knees in the snow and prayed, "Oh God, I just didn't understand. I just didn't understand."

That is what happened in the incarnation. The God of the universe entered time and space so that we might understand. God spoke clearly, directly, and lovingly.

One time Donald Barnhouse had preached in Boston, and a young preacher was very impressed. He approached Barnhouse and asked, "Dr. Barnhouse, how long did it take you to prepare that sermon?"

Barnhouse smiled and said, "It took twenty years and five minutes."

Father, how long did it take You to speak in Christ?

And He answered, "My child, it took thousands of centuries—and thirty-three years."

4   A HERITAGE OF PURPOSE

If Jesus has come...
the record has reason.

I am the Alpha and the Omega, the first and the last, the beginning and the end.

Revelation 22:13

It is easy to be pessimistic about human history. When you examine history in a superficial way, you can understand Edward Gibbon's comment, made after a lifetime of writing history, that history is "little more than the crimes, follies, and misfortunes of mankind." Voltaire's rather cynical evaluation of history reflects what anyone must feel after reading a number of different philosophies and versions of history. He said, "History is but a pack of tricks we play on the dead."

For a while I want to talk to you about history, and I suspect that the first thing you want to say is that you have already gotten enough history from the last chapter. But before you skip what follows, let me say a couple of things that might help. If you are like me, you found history rather boring in high school or college. The most important thing about history books was that the people in them were all dead. What could dead people possibly have to say to those of us who are alive? If you were like me, you memorized the dates, the battles, and the names and gave them back to the teacher on the exam, then promptly forgot them all as irrelevant and unimportant.

I am a lot older now and a little bit wiser, and do you know what I have found? History isn't as dry as I thought it was. In fact, I have found that the things I think, believe, and appreciate are deeply rooted in the history of my culture. But more important than that, I have found that Christians simply cannot afford to avoid history except at their own peril. The church didn't begin with Jimmy Swaggart or Martin Marty. More often than not, superficial Christians are people who have no sense of heritage and purpose. They are often Christians who never think about anything except how the Christian faith will make them happy and well.

I like to read C. S. Lewis's science fiction. It opens my mind to think of God as more than a nice deity who helps me with my mortgage payment. His science fiction allows me to see God as the God of the universe whose power and greatness force me to stand in awe and wonder and praise. Little gods have little worshipers, and when big, bad things happen to little worshipers, those worshipers fall apart.

In order for us Christians to stand against the new, lusty, materialistic paganism that is now running rampant across the world, we must have a world view that is as big as the God we worship. If we don't, we will be eaten alive. There is probably no better place for a Christian to develop a greater world view than in the study of history and God's part in it.

Now don't get me wrong. I have no vested interest in seeing you become a historian. I couldn't care less whether you can repeat facts and dates to Joe Pagan. I still have trouble with all of that. But I do want you to develop a view of history that will honor the God you worship. I want Christians, myself included, to have a view of God that won't crumble when the first thoughtful pagan utters an angry protest.

I am writing this in a friend's apartment that overlooks the ocean. Occasionally I look up from the typewriter and hear the crashing waves and look at the magnificent blue water. When I do, I remember the greatness and power of God. It helps when I go back to the typewriter. Just so, we Christians need sometimes to look up from the mundane (though necessary) living of our lives. We need to look at a God who is greater than anything we can imagine. When we go back to the tasks of "just keeping on keeping on," we then will be refreshed with new meaning and purpose.

Some of what follows may seem difficult. But stay with me

because it is important. History is important because what we think about ourselves is reflected in the way we think about history, and the way we think about history will reflect what future generations think about themselves. In other words, history books are not objective records of past events. History books reflect a philosophy of history, and that philosophy of history reflects what the generation writing the history values and reveres.

The Subjectivity of History

We live in a time when Christians are questioning the secular humanism in the public school system. The questions being asked are good ones, but I would suggest we ask many more questions about our history books. Future generations will be affected far more by history than by science. Science books are old almost as soon as they are written. In fact, if you want to get your library down to size, throw away every science book you have that is more than ten years old. We don't throw away history books because we have somehow come to the conclusion that a history book, no matter how old it is, is always good because it is an objective record of events that happened previously.

To be perfectly honest with you, however, there has never been an objective history book. Lucian, the Greek satirist of the second century A.D., said about history that "facts are not to be collected at haphazard, but with careful, laborious, repeated investigation." He was writing Philo about the subject, and he went on to say, "History abhors the intrusion of any least scruple of falsehood; it is like the windpipe, which the doctors tell us will not tolerate a morsel of stray food."

Now, Lucian sounds good until you read further and find that he recommended selectivity about the facts of history. In order to select properly, Lucien said we need "political insight." And where can we get "political insight"? Lucian said it is a gift of nature that "can never be learned." As a matter of fact, the "political insight" about which Lucian spoke is nothing more or less than a subjective philosophy of history.

In ancient civilizations, we find that history begins to be written almost as soon as the appearance of writing itself. When you examine the records of Egypt, China, and Mesopotamia, you find that conquering kings wanted to record their successes for later generations to read. You could hardly expect their records, commissioned and paid for by egotistical kings, to be objective. The organizing principle of the history books was the public relations of the king. Some six thousand years later, things haven't changed in the writing of history as much as you would think. There is always an organizing principle or philosophical view that affects what is recorded.

I am not saying that there are no facts in history books, nor am I saying that historians deliberately distort facts. While there are historians who do distort them, there are many more historians who are conscientious. There are both responsible and irresponsible historians, just as there are both responsible and irresponsible scientists, preachers, and secretaries. But the writing of history is not just the stringing together of facts. It involves two other important principles: philosophy, the historian's principle for organizing the historical data, and selection, the historian's principle for choosing from the vast data of history what he or she will record. No historian goes to his task without some kind of philosophy, and that philosophy determines the "facts" that will be used.

The ancient view that history is cyclical and the modern view that history is evolutionary are both philosophies that affect the writing of history. G. K. Chesterton's comment that Buddha is usually portrayed with his eyes closed because there is nothing important to see lends insight to the Eastern view of history; external events simply are unimportant. Hegel's idealistic dialectic and Karl Marx's materialistic dialectic both have tried to describe history as an evolutionary movement. That is, I would suggest, an amazing, illogical leap of faith that makes the faith of the Christian a very small thing. But, be that as it may, it is a philosophy, or organizing principle, of Marxian history. And then there are those modern historians who say that history has no meaning, and that assertion itself is their organizing principle. Whatever the philosophy—whether it is static (cyclical), upwardly evolutionary (H. G. Wells), or downwardly evolutionary (Oswald Spengler)—it is universally true that any history book reflects a world view with an organizing principle that attempts to give meaning to history.

The Bible's Philosophy of History

I have taken the time to write the above in order to say that the Bible also has a philosophy of history. A cursory reading of the Bible will show the reader that the Judeo-Christian faith is historical. In other words, the Bible is not primarily a book of doctrine or of philosophy; it is the record of God's actions in history. When liberals try to remove from the Bible the reality of actual past and future events, they cut out the very heart of the biblical faith.

The Bible proclaims from the beginning to end that history is "His story." If you want to know what God has done in the past, read a history book or, better, read the history recorded in the Bible. If you want to know what God is doing right now, read the newspapers, and if you want to know what God is going to do in the future, read prophecy. God is the God of history, and any attempt to understand Judaism or Christianity apart from that fact is futile.

The Christian faith proclaims that the God who is both outside of and yet involved in history has entered history Himself. He has intersected time and space not just to control history but to interact with history in a specific person, a Jew by the name of Jesus.

John's joy in that discovery is certainly understandable:

> What was from the beginning, what we have heard, what we have seen with our eyes, what we beheld and our hands handled, concerning the Word of Life—and the life was manifested, and we have seen and bear witness and proclaim to you the eternal life, which was with the Father and was manifested to us—what we have seen and heard we proclaim to you also, that you also may have fellowship with us; and indeed our fellowship is with the Father, and with His Son Jesus Christ. And these things we write, so that our joy may be made complete. (1 John 1:1-4)

And thus, Christians have an organizing principle of history, and that organizing principle is Jesus Christ. Oscar Cullman suggested that the biblical view of history does not reckon time in a continuous succession of events moving forward from one point to another. Rather, he suggested biblical history starts at the center, Jesus Christ, and moves backward and forward from that Christ event. James Boice said in his book *God and History*, "The appearance of Jesus was the decisive intervention of God in history. It gave the conclusive meaning to history as well as the basis for judgment upon it."[1]

And you say, "So what?" I'm going to tell you soon (and the answers are exciting), but let me first show you how the Bible views Christ as the organizing principle of history.

The book of Romans is perhaps the longest and most complete statement of Christianity's organizing principle. Paul showed that from the beginning God was working out a plan.

> For the wrath of God is revealed from heaven against all ungodliness and unrighteousness of men, who suppress the truth in unrighteousness, because that which is known about God is evident within them; for God made it evident to them. *For since the creation of the world* His invisible attributes, His eternal power and divine nature, have been clearly seen, being understood through what has been made, so that they are without excuse. (Rom. 1:18–20, emphasis added)

Then Paul narrowed history down to what is recorded in the Bible: "Nevertheless death reigned from Adam until Moses, even over those who had not sinned in the likeness of Adam's offense, who is a type of Him who was to come" (Rom. 5:14). Then Paul pointed to the Christ event:

> So then as through one transgression there resulted condemnation to all men, even so through one act of righteousness there resulted justification of life to all men. For as through the one man's disobedience the many were made sinners, even so through the obedience of the One the many will be made righteous. And the Law came in that the transgression might increase; but where sin

1. James Montgomery Boice, *God and History* (Downers Grove, Ill.: InterVarsity Press, 1981), p. 22.

increased, grace abounded all the more, that, as sin reigned in death, even so grace might reign through righteousness to eternal life through Jesus Christ our Lord. (Rom. 5:18–21)

Paul then pointed to the reason for creation and history:

> For the anxious longing of the creation waits eagerly for the revealing of the sons of God. For the creation was subjected to futility, not of its own will, but because of Him who subjected it, in hope that the creation itself also will be set free from its slavery to corruption into the freedom of the glory of the children of God. For we know that the whole creation groans and suffers the pains of childbirth together until now. (Rom. 8:19–22)

Matthew said that Jesus taught the people in parables "so that what was spoken through the prophet might be fulfilled, saying, 'I will open My mouth in parables; I will utter things *hidden since the foundation of the world*' " (Matt. 13:35, emphasis added). Paul wrote in Ephesians, "He made known to us the mystery of His will, according to His kind intention which He proposed in Him [i.e. Christ] with a view to an administration suitable to the fulness of the times, that is, the summing up of all things in Christ, things in the heavens and things upon the earth" (Eph. 1:9–10). After His baptism by John, Jesus said, "The time is fulfilled, and the kingdom of God is at hand; repent and believe in the gospel" (Mark 1:15).

The New Testament proclaims the glad news that the world has received the God of history into time and space. The followers of Christ knew that they had found the key to everything that had ever happened, that was happening, and that ever would happen in the world. Their organizing principle was absolute, and from Eusebius to Augustine to Schaff, "proper" history has been written because their philosophy of history was correct. Jesus of Nazareth is what history is all about.

In the fifteenth chapter of John, Jesus made an amazing statement. He said, "I am the true vine" (v. 1). His claim does not seem radical until you know the background of the statement. Jesus was not speaking in a vacuum. He was a Jew, using Jewish imagery, speaking to Jews about a Jewish concept.

Let me show you the background of the statement made by

Jesus. In Psalm 80 we read these words: "Thou didst remove a *vine* from Egypt; thou didst drive out the nations, and didst plant it. Thou didst clear the ground before it, and it took deep root and filled the land" (vv. 8–9). "O God of hosts, turn again now, we beseech Thee; look down from heaven and see, and take care of this vine" (v. 14). Isaiah said, "For the vineyard of the LORD of hosts is the house of Israel, and the men of Judah His delightful plant" (Isa. 5:7). Jeremiah added his testimony: "Yet I planted you a choice vine, a completely faithful seed. How then have you turned yourself before Me into the degenerate shoots of a foreign vine?" (Jer. 2:21). Ezekiel's testimony pointed to the same concept: "Your mother was like a vine in your vineyard, planted by the waters; it was fruitful and full of branches because of abundant waters" (Ezek. 19:10). Finally, listen to what the prophet Hosea said: "Israel is a luxuriant vine" (Hos. 10:1).

Now do you see it? When Jesus said that He was the true vine, the passages above came to the mind of His followers. Just as when someone talks of an eagle and citizens of the United States think of their country, so did His Jewish listeners think of Israel when Jesus talked of being the true vine. During the Maccabean period, the coinage of Israel was imprinted with a vine, just as many of the coins of the United States are imprinted with an eagle.

Jesus was saying, then, in the context of the Old Testament: "I am the essence of the nation of Israel; I am the prototype of which Israel is a type; I am the personification of everything Israel was created to be."

That is why, incidentally, the persecution by Jews of Christians in the first and second centuries was so horrible. Jesus was exactly what the Jews had been called to be. In Calvin Miller's *The Singer*, the Singer, Christ, had healed a madman, and the madman had been chained up to watch the torture and death of the Singer. The madman looked away because "he could not look upon the suffering of the only man who knew him sane."[2]

---

2. Calvin Miller, *The Singer* (Downers Grove, Ill.: InterVarsity Press. 1978), p. 112.

There are numerous reasons for anti-Semitism, but an important one is the fact that Jews are different. They are different because of their obedience to the Holy Torah, the law of God. They were laughed at and cursed by a world that didn't understand. And Jesus came to say, "The Jews are right, and they have been right all along." A rabbi friend of mine told me once that he was glad for Jesus. I asked him why, and he said, "Because Jesus introduced so many Gentiles to Judaism."

But the personification of Israel in Jesus is also the reason anti-Semitism is so horrible. For Christians, it borders on self-hatred. In *The Oath*, Elie Wiesel quotes the Talmud: "Had the peoples and the nations known how much harm they brought upon themselves by destroying the temple of Jerusalem, they would have wept more than the children of Israel."[3] Persecution of Jews by Christians is beyond understanding, given the personification of all Jews in Jesus.

If you want to understand the world, look at the Old Testament. The Old Testament gives the whole philosophy of history: God is the creator and sustainer of history. He started it, He will bring His purpose from it, and He will bring it to a close when that purpose is decided. But if you want to understand the Old Testament, you have to look at Jesus. He is the explanation of God's words in history. You want to know what the church is to be like, look at Jesus. You want to know where history is moving, look at Jesus. He is the organizing principle behind everything God ever intended to do in the world.

The Difference Jesus Makes

Now I move the previous question: so what? What difference does the Christian make? First, if Christ is the organizing principle, we know something about history's past. History is not just a series of events without meaning and without purpose. History has been created by a creator who has visited His creation.

---

3. Elie Wiesel, *The Oath* (New York: Random House, 1973), cover page.

Herbert Schlossberg has an interesting observation in his very good book *Idols for Destruction*:

> The modern historical profession is Hegelian in the sense that it assumes that the explanation of history lies within itself. Just as the antithesis lies within the thesis and the synthesis within the relationship between the two, so the meaning of history is thought to be comprehended exhaustively in itself. What the historian is unable to explain must be a matter of defective or incomplete sources or of his own limitations in drawing inferences from them. His failure to acknowledge that the explanation of history may lie outside of history is analogous to the naturalism of the physical and biological sciences, which all sees "the whole show" in the artifacts of creation. There is no evidence for this point of view, but being an assumption, it can live without evidence. The historians who hold it—most historians, that is—would express bewilderment that it should seriously be questioned. Even those historians who explicitly disbelieve it—Christians, for example—write history as if they do believe it. They are stretching the necessarily artificial boundaries of an academic discipline to encompass all of reality, accepting assumptions as professionals that they do not accept as individuals.[4]

In other words, Christian thinking about history ought to be quite different from that of our unbelieving friends. The Bible says, "In the beginning God created" (Gen. 1:1a). The psalmist said, "Know that the Lord Himself is God; it is He who has made us, and not we ourselves" (Ps. 100:3a). Again, "Of old Thou didst found the earth; and the heavens are the work of Thy hands" (Ps. 102:25).

As I was growing up I didn't care much about my family's history. But as I get older, I find myself interested in my family's roots. When our father died, my brother and I started asking questions about our background. We went to a number of towns in the mountains of North Carolina to talk to people who knew about our background. We visited our grandmother's grave (a woman we never knew) and a country store where our forefathers had worked. We walked across the land where our

4. Herbert Schlossberg, *Idols for Destruction* (Nashville: Thomas Nelson, 1983), pp. 23–24.

relatives had walked, and we visited the little mountain school our father had attended. It had not been important before, but when we realized that time was passing and that self-identity is important, we began to check into ours. We asked the older members of our family to tell us their memories, and we traced our mountain relatives back as far as we possibly could.

Our feelings that evening were changed. We felt a sense of satisfaction as we talked about our past and remembered the hardworking mountain people who had given us the present. We felt good about ourselves; we were able to define ourselves, and we were able to claim an identity because of the knowledge of our past.

Knowing how history started should give the thoughtful Christian feelings that are not dissimilar to those my brother and I experienced. History's creator is God, and that means that we are not animals or accidents of nature or dust. We are creatures with a past given to us by God. It is the answer to the meaningless drivel that says all of history is darkness—the darkness of the womb to the darkness of the grave. Not so; the creator has come to lay claim to His creation. That's really good news.

A Christian historian can never see history as a meaningless string of events. A Christian historian approaches his discipline with reverence and prayer, because he knows he is engaged in the study of God's hand as it molds, directs, and shapes history for His own purposes.

Second, if Christ is the organizing principle of history, we know something about the present. It is important. Throughout the history of the Christian church, there have been those who try to escape the reality of living. One Christian school advertised that it was one hundred miles from any known sin, reflecting a tendency among Christians that is neither biblical nor helpful. It is the kind of attitude that suggests the world is bad, bad, bad, and that Christians who are *really* Christians will always be trying to escape it.

One of the early Christian heresies was the heresy of Docetism (from the Greek word *dokeo*, meaning "to seem or to appear"). The Docetists taught that Jesus only appeared to be a man. He didn't really come in dirty flesh; it was only the *appearance* of reality. The Docetists taught that the world and the flesh are evil, and therefore it was unthinkable that Christ would really enter the world in human flesh.

That heresy has been floating around the church in one form or another ever since Marcion and the Gnostics first taught it in the early history of the church. You will find it in the philosophy of the Desert Fathers, who could not abide the sinful world of human relationships and went into the desert to be alone with God. You will find it in the escapist songs that are still sung in the church. You can find it in the fundamentalism of those whose separatist views call them to go only to Christian movies, watch only Christian television, wear only Christian sunglasses, go to only Christian schools, eat only Christian cookies, and wear only Christian underwear. You can find it in the heart of a Christian man or woman who has no unbelieving friends, or in the superficial Christian thinker who believes that politics is somehow dirty and beneath the concern of the Christian.

When John said that the Word had "become flesh," he was once and forever making a statement about the importance and reality of the world. It is not beyond redemption; it is the focus of God's concern. It is the territory to which the Christian, following the footsteps of Jesus, is called. An uninvolved, uncaring Christian is a contradiction.

One of the problems with the Christian church is that it often becomes militarily defensible. We have pulled in our troops and raised the drawbridge. If we can just defend the castle, "they" won't get us. How different from the message of Jesus! After the confession of Peter, He said, "Upon this rock I will build My church; and the gates of Hades shall not overpower it" (Matt. 16:18). In other words, have you ever been attacked by a gate? Jesus doesn't call us to retreat; He calls us to the battle for a world that is important. Our obedience should find expression in politics, in the arts, in education—in every area of the world—because Christ's coming has declared the world important.

One time Congressman Jack Kemp was asked if a Christian could be a politician. He replied with another question, "Can a

Christian not be a politician?" He had a point, and it was a biblical point. Present history must include the involvement of the Christian.

Finally, if Christ is the organizing principle of history, we know something about future history: it will end properly. I believe it was the historian Charles Beard who replied thusly to the question of what he had learned from history: "I have learned that those whom the gods would destroy they first make mad, that the bee fertilizes the flower from which it robs, that when it is dark enough you can see the stars, and finally I have learned that the mills of God grind slowly, but they grind exceedingly fine." God is in charge of history; and because He created it and sustains it, history will come to a successful conclusion.

Paul wrote to the Corinthians,

> Behold, I tell you a mystery; we shall not all sleep, but we shall be changed, in a moment, in the twinkling of an eye, at the last trumpet; for the trumpet will sound, and the dead will be raised imperishable, and we shall be changed. For this perishable must put on the imperishable, and this mortal must put on immortality. But when this perishable will have put on the imperishable, and this mortal will have put on immortality, then will come about the saying that is written, "Death is swallowed up in victory. O death, where is your victory? O death, where is your sting?" The sting of death is sin, and the power of sin is the law; but thanks be to God who gives us the victory through our Jesus Christ. Therefore, my beloved brethren, be steadfast, immovable, always abounding in the work of the Lord, knowing that your toil is not in vain in the Lord. (1 Cor. 15:51–58)

After speaking about some of the signs of the end of the age, Jesus said, "And then the sign of the Son of Man will appear in the sky, and then all the tribes of the earth will mourn, and they will see the Son of Man coming on the clouds of the sky with power and great glory" (Matt. 24:30). After Jesus ascended into the heavens, an angel said to His disciples, "Men of Galilee, why do you stand looking into the sky? This Jesus, who has been taken up from you into heaven, will come in just the same way as you have watched Him go into heaven" (Acts 1:11).

John wrote to the seven churches in Revelation, "Behold, He is coming with the clouds, and every eye will see Him, even those who pierced Him; and all the tribes of the earth will mourn over Him. Even so, Amen" (Rev. 1:7).

I do a lot of traveling from my home in Miami, Florida. If you live in Florida, the best time to travel north is during the winter. One of the great joys I have is speaking to a conference in the cold north where there is ice and snow. Even as I speak, I think, *As soon as this is over, I'm going back to where it is warm, where the palm trees sway in the breeze and the sun is shining.* A Christian finds the future much like that. This world is a difficult place to serve; sometimes it requires hurt and suffering. It is a world that is important, a world much loved by God, but it can be a cold and bitter place, nevertheless. Our meaning, however, lies in the fact that Jesus has come. His coming pointed to the past, sanctified the present, and gave hope and meaning to the future. Jesus said, "These things I have spoken to you, that in Me you may have peace. In the world you have tribulation, but take courage; I have overcome the world" (John 16:33).

When the first steamship, the *Clermont*, was demonstrated, a great crowd of scoffers stood on the shore watching the strange craft trying to get up enough steam to move. Many in the crowd shouted, "She'll never start! She'll never start!" Nevertheless, to the astonishment of the scoffers, the boat began to move. But, after a moment of stunned silence, their cynicism simply changed their words. Then they shouted, "She'll never stop! She'll never stop!"

Some people scoff at the idea that time will stop when Christ returns. Peter spoke about the problem in his second letter:

> Know this first of all, that in the last days mockers will come with their mocking, following after their own lusts, and saying, "Where is the promise of His coming? For ever since the fathers fell asleep, all continues just as it was from the beginning of creation....But the day of the Lord will come like a thief, in which the heavens will pass away with a roar and the elements will be destroyed with intense heat, and the earth and its works will be burned up....But according to His promise we are looking for new heavens and a new earth, in which righteousness dwells.

Therefore, beloved, since you look for these things, be diligent to be found by Him in peace, spotless and blameless. (2 Pet. 3:3-4, 10, 13, 14)

In the next chapter, we are going to deal with the problem of personal meaning in the Christian's life. But for now I want you to think back and remember that a Christian's life can't be meaningful except in the context of a meaningful world. Having a meaningful view of history is mandatory to his having a meaningful view of life. When Jesus Christ is the organizing principle of history, he can realize the vastness of God's plan and, more important, he can see his part as meaningful and important. As I think about history and God's oversight in history, I see my part as a piece of the puzzle. When it is completed, I will be a part of that completeness.

Dr. C. Everett Koop, the Surgeon General of the United States, once spoke for the graduation ceremonies of the Shipley School. The graduating class consisted of seventy girls and one boy. Dr. Koop was eager to avoid the "ladies and gentlemen" problem, having only one gentleman present; so he had a specially prepared message for the lone boy. Before he went to the speaker's podium to speak, he walked down to the graduates and handed the young man an envelope, and then he returned to the podium to deliver his speech to the young women in the graduating class. The message he gave the young man was as follows: "I have advice for your past, your present, and your future. For your past, think fondly of the time you spent with these young ladies; you're the envy of many. For the present, revel in it. For the future, marry a girl who not only heard but listened to what I said today."

Jesus has a message for just the Christians in the world. As we look to the past, we must be pleased with a God who created history and gave a meaning to the process. For the present, we must revel in it. For the future, we must plan to be present at the marriage supper of the Lamb who was slain that history might have purpose.

5 A HERITAGE OF MEANING

If Jesus has come...
my life has meaning.

Whoever drinks of the water that I shall give him shall never thirst; but
the water that I shall give him shall become in him a well of water spring-
ing up to eternal life.

John 4:14

A midlife crisis is a time when a man or woman realizes that
time is limited and will run out some day. It is a time when he or
she realizes that life is finite and that the goals that were a part
of youthful dreaming are probably not going to be reached. It is
a time of transition between doing and thinking, between asking how and asking why, between moving from birth and moving toward death.

I'm forty-three years old, and I'm going through my midlife
crisis. I really didn't know you call it that until fairly recently
when I was speaking for a conference in West Virginia. Some
friends of mine had just purchased a Christian bookstore, and
they wanted me to see it. As I was browsing through the shelves
of books in the store, my friend reached to a shelf just above
where I was standing and said, "Oh Steve, I have the perfect
book for you." She handed me a book dealing with midlife crisis
and its attendant problems. I suspect I looked rather abashed
because my friend, who is quick on the uptake, said, "Oh, I
don't mean it's for you; I mean it will be helpful in your coun-
seling."

After I read the book, I finally had a name for an ailment
from which I had suffered most of my life. There is something
about putting a name to a problem that makes one feel better

about it. Of course, I had not solved the problem, but I had a name: "midlife crisis." I began to share my newly named problem, and "a funny thing happened to me on the way to the forum." I found that almost every thinking person I knew was going through a midlife crisis, and some of them weren't even in midlife.

I also found that a midlife crisis is an ancient disease. The psalmist described the symptoms quite adequately:

> Hear my prayer, O Lord!
> And let my cry for help come to Thee.
> Do not hide Thy face from me in the day of my distress;
> Incline Thine ear to me;
> In the day when I call answer me quickly.
> For my days have been consumed in smoke,
> And my bones have been scorched like a hearth.
> My heart has been smitten like grass and has withered away.
> Indeed, I forget to eat my bread.
> Because of the loudness of my groaning my bones cling to my
>   flesh.
> I resemble a pelican of the wilderness;
> I have become like an owl of the waste places.
> I lie awake, I have become like a lonely bird on a housetop.
>   (Ps. 102:1–7)

A midlife crisis is, of course, not a midlife crisis at all. It is just a crisis of meaning, and most of us do everything in our power to keep from going through the crisis. We sterilize everything from birth to death; we avoid any conversation that goes beyond the baseball scores; we ease the pain with drugs or booze; we turn away from every tragedy and hide from every hurt; we take every trauma and make a sit-com out of it; we cover every flaw with vitamins and make-up. We operate under the ancient principle that if we don't think about something, maybe it will go away.

One of the things I have noticed after many years of dealing with terminally ill people is that friends and family don't know what to say to the dying, so they don't say anything. Even doctors and nurses avoid going into the rooms of dying patients because they don't know what to do, and the death of a patient reminds them of their own eventual death.

A few months ago I was on a plane from Miami to Los Angeles. When the plane took off, the people in my section were, as I remember it, more boisterous than the general run of airline passengers. There was a group of six or eight young men who were going home after a business meeting in Miami. They were talking about what they were going to do when they got home and how much fun they had had away from home. Two teenage girls in front of me talked about boys. Among the passengers in this section was the usual mix of tired salespeople trying to sleep, parents trying to calm their children, and people, like me, making plans for whatever was going to happen in Los Angeles.

Then a woman screamed. It was not a moderate scream, either; it was bloodcurdling. She turned to the quickly approaching flight attendant and said through her sobs, "My daughter is dying!" For the next twenty minutes, three physicians culled from the passengers on the plane worked frantically on the teenage girl who slowly died in the aisle beside my seat. The pilot made an emergency landing in Dallas, and the sheet-draped body of the girl was taken off the plane accompanied by the sobbing mother.

I am not a stranger to death. No pastor is. I have stood by more deathbeds than I can count and have cleaned up after more suicides than I care to remember. Death is a reality with which a pastor is very familiar; so I was able to be rather objective about the tragic scene taking place on the airplane that day. I was not unmoved; I was simply able to stand back and observe the reactions of those around me. There was a strange, eerie silence on the rest of the trip to Los Angeles. The teenagers who had been talking about boys before were silently crying and embracing each other. The tired salespeople were no longer sleeping, and the men returning from their convention were trying to forget the scene they had just witnessed by consuming as many of the free drinks offered by the airline as they could get down. No one spoke, as each person on that airplane contemplated his own thoughts about tragedy and death.

Most of the time we can escape such thoughts. When we see death, we can turn away. But we were on an airplane, and nobody could leave. It was an interesting "controlled" experiment.

I had a strange desire to stand up and preach a sermon. Of course, I couldn't do that; but if I had, I can assure you I would have had a most attentive audience. In fact, a crisis is sometimes the best time to get people to listen to truth. If I could have preached a sermon that day, I would have said the things I am going to tell you in this chapter.

The Lessons of Ecclesiastes

One of my favorite books in the Bible is the book of Ecclesiastes. It is interesting to note the Christians who try to "explain away" the book because it doesn't fit into our crossless Christianity. The writer of Ecclesiastes was an ancient Albert Camus articulating the emptiness and meaninglessness of a world where God is the only hope. Listen to some of what he said:

> What advantage does man have in all his work which he does under the sun? A generation goes and a generation comes, but the earth remains forever. Also, the sun rises and the sun sets; and hastening to its place it rises there again. Blowing toward the south, then turning toward the north, the wind continues swirling along; and on its circular courses the wind returns. All the rivers flow into the sea, yet the sea is not full. To the place where the rivers flow, there they flow again. All things are wearisome; man is not able to tell it. The eye is not satisfied with seeing, nor is the ear filled with hearing. That which has been is that which will be, and that which has been done is that which will be done. So, there is nothing new under the sun....
>
> I, the Preacher, have been king over Israel in Jerusalem. And I set my mind to seek and explore by wisdom concerning all that has been done under heaven. It is a grievous task which God has given to the sons of men to be afflicted with. I have seen all the works which have been done under the sun, and behold, all is vanity and striving after wind. What is crooked cannot be straightened, and what is lacking cannot be counted. I said to myself, "Behold, I have magnified and increased wisdom more than all who were over Jerusalem before me; and my mind has ob-

served a wealth of wisdom and knowledge." And I set my mind to
know wisdom and to know madness and folly; I realized that this
also is striving after wind. Because in much wisdom there is much
grief, and increasing knowledge results in increasing pain. (1:3–9,
12–18)

And then after showing the emptiness of life, the Preacher
said, "Remember Him [God] before the silver cord is broken
and the golden bowl is crushed, the pitcher by the well is shattered and the wheel at the cistern is crushed; then the dust will
return to the earth as it was, and the spirit will return to God
who gave it. 'Vanity of vanities,' says the Preacher, 'all is vanity!' " (12:6–8).

Do you ever wonder why you do what you do? Do you sometimes think that you get up in the morning and go to work in order to make enough money to pay the mortgage and buy the
food so you will have a place to sleep and eat in order to get up
in the morning and go to work?

There is a great little book by Trina Paulus titled *Hope for the
Flowers*. It is one of those picture books for adults in the genre of
the Dr. Seuss books for children. The story traces the life of a
caterpillar named Stripe from birth to butterfly. When Stripe
was first born he tried to decide what to do with his life. He met
a girl caterpillar named Yellow, and for a while their relationship was enough to sustain Stripe. But eventually he began to
wonder if there was something more to life.

One day Stripe noticed a gigantic pillar, and on closer examination he realized it was a pillar of caterpillars stretching up
into the sky. As he looked closer he noted that the caterpillars
were climbing over one another trying to get to the top of the
pillar. And so Stripe began to climb, too.

"Stripe didn't seem just 'disciplined' to others—he seemed
ruthless. Even among climbers he was special. He didn't think
he was against anybody. He was just doing what he had to if he
was to get to the top. 'Don't blame *me* if you don't succeed! It's
a tough life. Just make up your mind,' he would have said had
any caterpillar complained."[1]

1. Trina Paulus, *Hope for the Flowers* (Paramus, N.J.:Paulist Press, 1972), p. 89.

It was difficult, but finally Stripe made it near the top of the pillar of caterpillars, where he found that no matter how hard he tried he couldn't get any higher. Then he heard someone above him say there was no way to get higher without getting rid of "them," and then the pillar began to shake and caterpillars began to scream and fall. Then there was silence.

> Frustration surged through Stripe. But as he was agreeing this was the only way up he heard a tiny whisper from the top: "There's nothing here at all!" It was answered by another: "Quiet fool! They'll hear you down the pillar. We're where *they* want to get. That's what's here!"
> Stripe felt frozen. To be so high and not high at all! It only looked good from the bottom. The whisper came again. "Look over there—another pillar—and there too—everywhere!" Stripe became angry as well as frustrated. "My pillar," he moaned, "only one of thousands. Millions of caterpillars climbing nowhere! Something is really wrong but...what else is there?"[2]

In Stripe's final question we see the anxiety of midlife crisis, adolescence crisis, and old-age crisis. What is life all about? Is this all there is? Is there something more than this pillar?

Now let's return to the book of Ecclesiastes. I suggest you stop reading right here, turn to that book in the Bible and read it. It's a short book of twelve chapters, and it is well worth your time. But reading it makes a question simmer in the back of your mind: why would God allow a book that seems so cynical and nihilistic to be in His revelation? I suspect there are five good reasons, and all of them must be understood before we turn to how the doctrine of the incarnation answers the problem of human meaninglessness.

First, God allowed Ecclesiastes to be written because it strikes to the very heart of the easy sentimentality and superficiality that so often plagues the people of God. Somehow Christians have adopted the idea that the world is the playground for God's people, a place where God's main business is to make people happy and His people's main business is to be happy.

President Robinson of Middleburn College told a graduat-

2. *Ibid.*, p. 94.

ing class one time, "You may have thought, having finished your finals and having turned in your last papers, that you now can see the light at the end of the tunnel. Well, dear friends, if you can see the light at the end of the tunnel, you are probably facing the wrong direction." Although it is cynical, that is good advice about the way the world really is. As a matter of fact, this world has sorrow, hurt, tragedy, and sickness. I don't like that any more than you do, but nevertheless, it is a fact.

Every once in a while someone asks me, "Pastor, are you happy?" Well, sometimes I'm happy and sometimes I'm not, but the question itself is irrelevant. God didn't put us in this world to be happy. That is where "prosperity theology" has made a great mistake. Faithful, consistent Christians do suffer. So either God is a monster and a liar or some of His teachers got their wires messed up. Don't believe anybody who tells you that it is always God's will for Christians to be healthy, wealthy, and wise. It didn't happen to Jesus, or to Paul, or to Peter. It probably won't happen to us, either. The book of Ecclesiastes reminds us that the way to meaning is not a dream world that doesn't exist.

Second, God allowed the book of Ecclesiastes to be included in the canon because it allows the believer to track on somebody else's experience, somebody who was extremely honest and wise. Have you ever been tempted to return to the world's ways in order to be happy? There are those times when I sit in my study after a day of listening to the hurt of my people, tired from trying to be faithful, tired from trying to be a teacher of things that are hard to understand and even harder to live. On those occasions I can empathize, if only a little bit, with the prophet Jeremiah. You will remember that he was the least successful man of God who ever lived. Everything he tried, failed; every time he told God's people to do one thing, they did another; every time he was faithful, everybody else seemed unfaithful. The people he was sent to serve tried to kill him. It is a monument to this great prophet and to God's grace that Jeremiah tenaciously persisted in his obedience to God.

Jeremiah pleaded his case before the Lord. He said, "Why has the way of the wicked prospered? Why are all those who deal in treachery at ease? Thou hast planted them, they have also taken root; they grow, they have even produced fruit" (Jer. 12:1–2).

I can understand Jeremiah, and I'll bet you can, too. Sometimes it just doesn't seem worth it to struggle. Well, when I start feeling that way, I turn to the book of Ecclesiastes, where I am able to see how empty and banal the way of the world really is. Then the world isn't so attractive and I think, "I don't need that. There is no meaning there."

A third probable reason God gave us the book of Ecclesiastes is that it enables us to deal with the ambiguity of life, with the fact that life appears simple but does not have simple answers. It helps us to see how important it is not to take life too seriously. I have a friend who says that in order to be a Christian in this world, one must have a tolerance for ambiguity. In other words, if we are to look for meaning, we must be very careful not to look for it in life.

Have you ever noticed how we Christians like systems? I used to preach a sermon on "The Five Ways to Know God's Will." A few years ago I was trying to discover God's will in a particular area of my life, and I went through all five of those ways I had been teaching. Do you know something? I still didn't know God's will! Trying to find meaning in systems can be devastating. You will find systems everywhere: The Four Steps to Salvation, How to Find Peace, Ten Rules for Parents, How to Save Your Marriage.

Don't get me wrong. I'm not saying there isn't truth to a lot of systems. I am simply saying that life doesn't fit into a neat, nice, compact system. If it did, there would be no problem finding life's meaning. The writer of Ecclesiastes said that life is filled with ambiguity, and that if you try to find your meaning by the resolution of the ambiguity, you are going to be disappointed. I have often seen people reject the Christian faith because they said it didn't work. They were simply wrong. Some nice system didn't work, which isn't the same thing as the Christian faith's not working.

A fourth reason for the book of Ecclesiastes is that it provides a warning for those who would reduce the Scriptures to humanistic secularism. Every once in a while, someone says to me about a friend, "He is a Christian, but he doesn't believe in God." In other words, he is telling me that so and so is a "good person." But the writer of Ecclesiastes said that a very good person and a very bad person have the same result: vanity.

Somehow we have believed the myth that "goodness is its own reward." Let me tell you something important: goodness is *not* its own reward. In fact, goodness is stupid if one is good without reference to God. Mark Twain said once that the church is a place where a nice, respectable person stands in front of other nice, respectable people and urges them to be nicer and more respectable. If that is all the church does, it is leading people down the wrong path. There is not meaning in goodness. Besides, how do we know that good is good?

Finally, the book of Ecclesiastes is included in God's book because it forces believers to the only source of meaning, God the Father. It is said that Alexander the Great once found an enemy soldier dying of cold and exposure. He had his servants bring the soldier into his tent and put him on his own bed until he was warm. When the man woke and noticed that he was in the king's bed, he became frightened. Alexander smiled and said, "To recline in the bed of the Macedonian king is death, but to recline in my bed is life." The writer of Ecclesiastes, in twelve chapters, pulled the slats out of all royal beds save One. He said, "The conclusion, when all has been heard, is: fear God and keep His commandments, because this applies to every person" (Eccles. 12:13).

John the Baptist's Example

There is a great record in Luke's gospel of a man who was searching for meaning. His name was John the Baptist, and he needed to know the truth because he was going to die; and he was afraid his death would prove to be meaningless. John was born to a priest named Zacharias and his God-fearing wife, Elizabeth, and he was consecrated in his mother's womb to be a servant of God.

As a young man, John went into the wilderness to begin the

ministry God had given him. If you had known John you might
not have liked him. He was not a good-old-boy-back-slapper;
he was a lightning bolt in the hand of the Almighty. He dressed
in camel hair, ate wild locusts, and was very earthy and direct.
His message was twofold: 1) you are sinners, and 2) you must
repent and be baptized. But more important than even the message was the fact that John was to prepare the way for the coming Messiah. In fact, John identified Jesus as the Messiah.

In the seventh chapter of Luke, John was awaiting his execu-
tion by Herod because he had challenged the king's immorality.
The pathos of the situation is almost overwhelming. John knew
he was going to die, but he didn't fear death. He feared instead
that his life had been lived in vain. He feared that Jesus wasn't
the Messiah after all, the One who had verified and given
meaning to John's ministry. In other words, John's problem
was not death; his problem was meaninglessness.

One of my favorite books is *Prayers*, by Michel Quoist, a
French priest. It contains some of the most beautiful and honest
prayers I have ever read. "It Is Dark" reflects the despair John
the Baptist must have felt in his final hours.

> Lord, it is dark.
> Lord, are you here in my darkness?
> Your light has gone out, and so has its reflection on me and on all
>   the things around me.
> Everything seems grey and somber as when a fog blots out the sun
>   and enshrouds the earth.
> Everything is an effort, everything is difficult, and I am heavy-
>   footed and slow.
> Every morning I am overwhelmed at the thought of another day. I
>   long for the end, I yearn for the oblivion of death.
> I should like to leave,
> Run away,
> Flee,
> Anywhere, escape.
> Escape what?
> You, Lord, others, myself, I don't know,
> But leave,
> Flee.
>
> I go along haltingly, like a drunkard,

From force of habit, unconsciously.
I go through the same motions each day, but I know that they are
    meaningless.
I walk, but I know that I am getting nowhere.
I speak, and my words seem dreadfully empty, for they can reach
    only human ears and not the living souls who are far above.
Ideas themselves escape me, and I find it hard to think.
I stammer, confused, blushing,
And I feel ridiculous
And abashed, for people will notice me.
Lord, am I losing my mind?
Or is all this what you want?

It wouldn't matter, except that I am alone.
I am alone.
You have taken me far, Lord; trusting, I followed you, and you
    walked at my side,
And now, in the middle of the desert, at night, suddenly you have
    disappeared.
I call, and you do not answer.
I search, and I do not find you.
I have left everything, and now am left alone.
Your absence is my suffering.

Lord, it is dark.
Lord, are you here in my darkness?
Where are you, Lord?
Do you love me still?
Or have I wearied you?
Lord, answer,
Answer!

It is dark.[3]

In his despair, John the Baptist did the only thing he knew to
do: he sent his disciples to Jesus with a list of questions—halting, hurting, helpless questions. "Jesus," they said, "John
wants to know...he is afraid, lonely, and facing death. John
wants to know about you. Are you the Messiah, or should we go
and search out another? Has John wasted his life and his ministry?"
    Perhaps you have had your periods of doubt and fear, too.

3. Michel Quoist, *Prayers* (New York: Sheed and Ward, 1963), pp. 139–140.

Perhaps you have wondered if life has meaning and have asked the same questions John asked. Jesus is still giving the answer He gave to John's crisis of meaning. He gave John and can give you meaning with a demonstration, a proposition, a commendation, and a declaration.

Jesus' Demonstration

Jesus' demonstration was this:

> At that very time He cured many people of diseases and afflictions and evil spirits; and He granted sight to many who were blind. And He answered and said to them, "Go and report to John what you have seen and heard: the blind receive sight, the lame walk, the lepers are cleansed, and the deaf hear, the dead are raised up, the poor have the gospel preached to them." (Luke 7:21-22)

If Jesus has come, there is meaning in life because in His coming and in His loving there is a demonstration of God's care for His people. If nothing more, the incarnation is the way the infinite breaks into the finite to demonstrate in time and space that there is meaning. If there is no God, there is no value; if there is no value, there is no meaning; if there is no meaning, then you are a turnip. But God has come and demonstrated His love for us.

He is still demonstrating His love for us in Christ. Not too long ago I was having my weekly pity party. I was feeling that my ministry was of little or no use to anyone. And then I got a long distance call from a Methodist minister in another state. He said, "Steve, you don't know me, but the Baptist minister in our town gave me some of your tapes. I would like to be placed on the Key Life Tape list, but, more than that, I wanted you to know that Jesus speaks through you, and I'm glad." And I thought I heard Jesus say to the angels, "Go tell Steve that the hungry are fed."

Last week I felt the world had come to an end. All my plans looked like Jericho after the trumpets; I had been criticized for an action that was well-intentioned; I had received a letter very critical of something I had written; one of my close friends had left the ministry and declared his atheism; and I found that a man had left the church I pastor angry about something I had said. I was at that point where you say, "What's the use?" And then I opened a letter that had been on my desk for most of the morning. It was from a dear Christian brother. He wrote, "Steve, I was praying for you this morning, and Jesus told me to write. Well, maybe that is a little too spiritual, but I did feel 'led' to write. I wanted you to know that I love you and the way God uses you in my life." And between the lines I saw the message from Jesus, "Go tell Steve he isn't alone."

I have been walking with Jesus for a long time, and He always has demonstrated His love for me. Sometimes He demonstrates His love through compassion in one of His friends. At other times His demonstration is a direct answer to a prayer, and sometimes His demonstration is in the simple form of a loving listener. There are times when my only comfort is Jesus Himself, and in those times I realize a truth from Ron Dunn: "A lot of people say, 'Jesus is all I need.' You will never know if Jesus is all you need, until Jesus is all you've got. When Jesus is all you've got, then you will know that Jesus is all you need."

It began in the incarnation. We don't find platitudes there or empty religious language. We asked: are you there? Do you love? How much do you love? And Jesus said, "I love you this much." And He stretched out His arms on a cross and died. That was the beginning of a pattern, a pattern that points to a God who is really there. If Jesus has come, there really is a God; if there really is a God, there is value; if there is value, there is meaning; and if there is meaning, I can keep on keeping on.

Jesus' Proposition

In the midst of John's fear of meaninglessness, Jesus called John to build on what he knew. He told John's messengers, "And blessed is he who keeps from stumbling over Me" (Luke 7:23). It's necessary to be familiar with a couple of messianic passages in the book of Isaiah to understand what Jesus was saying. In Isaiah 29:18, the prophet said, "And on that day the deaf shall hear words of a book, and out of their gloom and darkness the eyes of the blind shall see." In chapter thirty-five,

Isaiah spoke again, "Then the eyes of the blind will be opened, and the ears of the deaf will be unstopped. Then the lame will leap like a deer, and the tongue of the dumb will shout for joy. For waters will break forth in the wilderness and streams in the Arabah" (Isa. 35:5-6).

Remember two things: first, John was a man who knew the Scripture, and second, John used the title "messiah" based upon his knowledge of the Scripture. He meant by "messiah" a great political leader who would restore Israel to her place among the nations, restore righteousness on the earth, and restore respect for the name of God in the world.

You can imagine why John was confused. He had expected someone quite different from Jesus. He had expected a political and military figure, a great charismatic leader. But Jesus was none of those things, and it shook John to the foundations of his faith and meaning.

We, of course, have some data John didn't have. We know the two themes of messianic prophecy in the Old Testament. One deals with the coming "suffering servant," and the other deals with the political and military leader. We know that Jesus has already fulfilled the first in the incarnation and that He will fulfill the second upon His return. But John didn't know that, and thus his dilemma.

When Jesus told John's disciples to report what they had seen, He was saying, "John, please know that I am the Messiah but that I am fulfilling only half of the messianic prophecies. Your questions will have to wait, but I have answered enough of them to let you know that you haven't missed the road. Blessed is the person who doesn't stumble over [i.e., take offense at] Me."

The proposition to John as he faced meaninglessness was that he should not try to figure out everything and that he had enough to know the truth. Someone came to me not too long ago and said, "Steve, it must be wonderful to be a Bible teacher and to have the answers." I didn't tell my friend the whole truth then because he was a new Christian and he wasn't ready to hear it, but the truth is this: the more I walk with Jesus, the less sure I am of a lot of things—and the more sure I am of Him.

Let me give you a principle that will help you when you're confused: whatever you think God is doing in your life right now, He probably isn't. That principle helps me live with the paradox of trying to put God in a box. You see, He wants us to learn to trust Him no matter what happens. Meaning isn't to be found in having all questions answered, all problems solved, all ambiguity resolved. Meaning is found only in the fact that Jesus has come. If that is true, then the rest will be okay.

Jesus' Commendation

Look at Luke 7:26–28a: "But what did you go out to see? A prophet? Yes, I say to you, and one who is more than a prophet. This is the one about whom it is written, 'Behold, I send My messenger before Your face, who will prepare Your way before You.' I say to you, among those born of women, there is no one greater than John." In other words, "John, as confused and frightened as you are, you are doing it right!"

A number of months ago, I was having problems trying to balance my work as a pastor with my writing and my outside speaking engagements. God has blessed me with a very affirming and loving congregation of believers at Key Biscayne, who have never tried to force me into some kind of false ministerial role. My problem was the guilt I was feeling about the whole situation; there was no fault in the people or the leadership of the church. I decided I needed some advice from someone who had dealt successfully with the problem; so I called Stuart Briscoe. The advice he gave me was very wise and helpful. He asked me some questions and listened to the answers, and then he said, "Steve, you are doing it right, but you will probably still feel guilty." I have thought about what he said on more than one occasion when I was feeling guilty. I have been able to deal with the guilt because a man I respect told me that, at least in this one area, I was doing it right.

The incarnation of Christ enables us to know what the right track is, even when we don't feel very good about it. Longfellow's lines certainly don't apply to all models, but if they apply to the Son of God they are quite appropriate:

Lives of great men all remind us
We can make our lives sublime,
And, departing, leave behind us
Footprints on the sands of time;
Footprints, that perhaps another,
Sailing o'er life's solemn main,
A forlorn and shipwrecked brother,
Seeing, shall take heart again.[4]

The old spiritual speaks to the issue when it says, "You done showed us how." In the incarnation, Jesus showed us how; He gave us a model of following the God of the universe. He commends us when we conform to that model, and in the conformity and the affirmation there is meaning. The most meaningful words in the world come from His lips: "Well done, good and faithful slave" (Matt. 25:21).

Jesus' Declaration

Jesus concluded His references to John by saying, "For John the Baptist has come eating no bread and drinking no wine; and you say, 'He has a demon!' The Son of Man has come eating and drinking; and you say, 'Behold, a gluttonous man, and a drunkard, a friend of tax-gatherers and sinners!' Yet wisdom is by all her children" (Luke 7:33–35). In other words, Jesus was saying, "It will all come out in the wash!"

In Jeremiah 32, Jeremiah was called by God to purchase a field in Anathoth. That was not an unusual thing to do, but in this case the Chaldean army was preparing to invade, and the property was soon going to be worthless. Jeremiah went to a man by the name of Hanamel and asked to purchase the property. Hanamel thought Jeremiah was a fool, but Hanamel was not one to pass up a good deal even if it did come from a fool.

Jeremiah explained why he bought the property: "Thus says the Lord of hosts, the God of Israel, 'Take these deeds, this sealed deed of purchase, and this open deed, and put them in an

---

4. Henry Wadsworth Longfellow, from the poem "A Psalm of Life," quoted in *Major American Writers*, Jones, Leisy & Ludwig, eds. (New York: Harcourt, Brace and Company, 1952), p. 581.

earthenware jar, that they may last a long time.' For thus says the Lord of hosts, the God of Israel, 'Houses and fields and vineyards shall again be bought in this land' " (Jer. 32:14–15).

History has a way of vindicating bad guys; Jeremiah looked to the future and knew the truth. Jesus' coming declared that every act of obedience, every prayer, every bit of suffering for righteousness' sake is taken into account in the economy of God. God does balance His books, and because He does, a wrong road will go to the wrong place, and a right road will go to the right place. The road always ends in the place where it leads. The ambiguity is still there, but hang tough because Jesus has promised. If He has come, then life has meaning.

Newspapers have a way of being cynical. Cynicism is sometimes needed, but I think the writers of an editorial in a Chicago paper went a bit too far: "The cheek of every American must tingle with shame as he reads the silly, dish-watery utterances of a man who has to be pointed out to intelligent foreigners as the President of the United States."

Perhaps, like John, you are sitting around wondering if there is any real meaning to your life. Perhaps you find yourself wondering if, given the hatred and the helplessness of the world, you ought to join the cynics. That is understandable. Sometimes I feel that way, too. But it isn't going to happen with me, because God has promised that all who follow Christ will shine like the sun.

John knows that now. In fact, he knew it for sure shortly after he received his message from Jesus. He was executed, and at that very second he stood in the throne room of the God of the universe. I suspect that God laughed and said, "John, I told you so."

Oh yes. That editorial from the Chicago newspaper. It was written in 1865 in the Chicago *Times*. It was in reference to Abraham Lincoln's "Gettysburg Address." Things do have a way of coming out in the wash.

6 A HERITAGE OF VICTORY

If Jesus has come...
Satan can't win.

The Son of God appeared for this purpose, that He might destroy the works of the devil.

1 John 3:8b

If you are typical, you will react to what I have to say in the pages of this chapter in one of two ways: either you will laugh it off as the silly musings of an outdated religionist, or you will turn to this chapter first because you are both fascinated by and afraid of the idea and person of Satan. Both of those reactions are inappropriate. In fact, they represent the two great dangers into which Christians can fall when dealing with the subject of Satan.

There was a time in my life when I was tempted by the first of those extremes. I simply couldn't bring myself to believe that there could be personal evil in the world, far less that it was called Satan. You see, I was an intellectual, and intellectuals are far too sophisticated to hold some medieval view of a wicked man running around in a weird, red suit carrying a pitchfork. Oh yes, I delighted in discussing Goethe's *Faust*. We intellectuals could deal with the character of Mephistopheles without sacrificing our intellectual credibility. Dante's Lucifer and Milton's Satan, by far the most attractive characters in *The Inferno* and

Paradise Lost, were safe, but to discuss a real, live devil was simply beyond consideration.

Sometimes when I need to be humbled before God, I reread some of the sermons I preached right after I graduated from seminary. Those sermons make me blush. The people in the first church I served were very forgiving of their young pastor, but there are many times I wish I could go back to that little church on Cape Cod and apologize for some of the things I taught those dear people.

There is one sermon in particular that I sometimes read. I was just out of seminary and was preaching on the temptations of Jesus. As you know, Satan is a prominent figure in the accounts of Jesus' temptations. In that sermon I had great difficulty referring to him as "Satan" or the "devil." So, do you know what I did? Whenever it became necessary to refer to Satan, I called him the "metaphorical personification of evil."

One time Albert Schweitzer was doing some manual labor at his hospital at Lambaréné. A native was watching, and Schweitzer asked him to help. The native refused, saying that he was not a common laborer but an intellectual. Schweitzer turned back to his work, saying, "Once I thought I was an intellectual, too." Well, once I thought I was an intellectual, and that thought prevented me from seeing a lot of truths, among them the reality, personality, and power of Satan.

There is the other extreme of seeing Satan around every corner and under every bed. Probably at no time in the history of the church has so much been written about Satan. A lot of the literature is helpful, but much of it is plain silly. Be that as it may, with the publicity Satan has been getting lately, some folks have gone "Satan happy." Satan and his demons are everywhere. If you sin, the devil made you do it. If you are angry, you have a "spirit" of anger. And if you can't quit smoking, your problem isn't that you lack discipline; your problem is that you have a demon of addiction.

In a congregation I once served, there developed a fascination with demons and demonology, and one Sunday morning I left my notes (I always get into trouble when I leave my notes) to speak to the issue. Among other things, I said, "Some of you are so fascinated by Satan that you have taken your eyes off God, and a lot of your frustration is nothing more or less than silly superstition. One of these days some of you are going to meet a real demon, and it is going to scare your socks off." I was told later that some people were angry at me, and one couple walked out of the church never to return. I wish the couple had come back to the church because my remarks were not as loving as they ought to have been, but what I said needed to be heard. Satan gets a lot of mileage out of the Christian's fear, and it is from gasoline for which he didn't pay. Rumors of Satan's power are far greater than its reality, and it is time Christians realized that.

It is said that Samuel Rutherford, the seventeenth-century Scottish clergyman, once heard a noise in his sitting room. It was the middle of the night, and Rutherford decided to check it out. He climbed out of bed and went to the sitting room. He found Satan, as big as life, sitting in his favorite chair. Rutherford laughed and said, "Oh, it's only you" and went back to bed to sleep.

In the next few pages I have some bad news and some good news for you. The bad news is that Satan is very real and he is out to get you. The good news is that because Jesus has come, Satan is a defeated foe. As someone has said, "The dragon has been slain, but his tail still swishes." Before we go any farther, let's consider the bad news.

The Reality of Satan

There is a devil and I have seen him. I have seen him walking down the streets of a city slum; I have watched him do his work with a needle dripping heroin; I have seen him in a bottle clutched in the hand of a drunk asleep on a bench on Boston Common. I have seen Satan's handwriting in a suicide note, and I have noticed his smile as crowds lined up to watch an "adult" movie. I have seen the work of Satan in a crushed automobile, an empty stomach, and a dead soldier. I have seen Satan in the words of a man who said he didn't need God and in the sneer of a woman who was asked if she knew Christ. I have seen Satan in the hurt, emptiness, and frustration of humanity. Sometimes I see him in my doubts, my depression, my lust, my anger, and my fear.

The writers of the Bible didn't mind talking about Satan at all. They called him the liar, the accuser, the dragon, the serpent, and the ruler of the world. What the Bible says about the work of Satan is enough to make any believer pause. Satan is the tempter who would lure the believer away from the walk of faith. He seeks to destroy God's Word in the experience of the believer. He is an accuser who would cripple the Christian with guilt and fear. He sometimes becomes dominant in an individual life either in person or through one of his minions. Satan is responsible for sin and unbelief, and he rejoices whenever he can turn a pagan away from Christ and a Christian away from the truth. He would have you fall down and worship him even if you call him by another name. He is real; he is alive; and he is dangerous.

Marshall Fishwick wrote in *Faust Revisited*, "There are those today who do not believe in the Devil. They are the first fallen: for Satan always begins by trying to convince us that he doesn't exist. The wisest human minds, and the God made Man, have acknowledged the existence of the forces of evil, and wrestled with them. So must we."[1]

If you are having trouble believing in the reality of the devil, let me say a couple of things to you. First, truth and reality have an uncomfortable tendency to defy both systems and convention. The proper searcher after truth isn't limited by his own presuppositions. In other words, don't let your preconceived ideas of Satan and those who believe in Satan get in the way of truth. In the words of Hamlet as he spoke to Horatio, both of whom had just seen a ghost, "There are more things in heaven and earth, Horatio, than are dreamt of in your philosophy."

1. Marshall W. Fishwick, *Faust Revisited, Some Thoughts on Satan* (New York: The Seabury Press: 1963), p. 4.

One of the most interesting texts in the entire Bible is found in 1 Samuel 28. King Saul, who had outlawed all mediums, decided that he needed to see one. In desperation he visited a witch in Endor. Now the thrust of the text is that the old witch was a charlatan. People really believed she talked to the spirits of the dead, and she laughed all the way to the bank.

Saul went to her and said, "Call up Samuel!" Samuel was the dead prophet of God, and the old woman, having gone through her routine often, began to get out her bag of tricks. And then, to her horror, old Samuel appeared. Now, dear reader, that is enough to shake the false teeth out of a mound of Poli–Grip. The text reads, "When the woman saw Samuel, she cried out with a loud voice" (1 Sam. 28:12). You would have, too. It was rather traumatic to have all her presuppositions shattered so quickly. That old witch was simply confronted with a reality she couldn't explain.

Before you laugh at the Bible's teaching on the reality and the personality of Satan, I suggest you look over your shoulder. Before you erase the supernatural from your vocabulary, please make sure your dictionary is not out of date. Time after time, I have seen Christians absolutely devastated because they disregarded the clear teaching of the Bible on the person of Satan. When they had an encounter with him, they were not prepared to deal with his reality.

And that brings me to the other thing I want to say to you about Satan: information from Scripture that you find difficult to accept ought to be filed away or put on the back burner for a while. The time will come when that information will be of great value. Nothing is included in Scripture that wasn't meant to be there, and all of it, including the doctrine of Satan, was given that we might "be adequate [i.e., mature], equipped for every good work" (2 Tim. 3:17).

Did you hear about the corn farmer who decided to become a chicken farmer? He went to the feed store and ordered a hundred baby chicks. A week passed and he came back into the same feed store and ordered another hundred. The owner of the feed store said, "Why in the world do you need another hundred? What happened?" The farmer said, "The first hundred died, and I can't figure out why. I'm either planting them too deep or watering them too much." You see, the problem was that the farmer tried to transfer his knowledge of corn farming over to chicken farming, and it just didn't work.

Christians who try to deal with the supernatural world by using natural laws have the same problem. One of the interesting things about Jesus is the way He reverses so much of what we think is true. He says that we are to love our enemies and pray for those who persecute us. He says that if we want to lead we have to serve; if we want to find our lives we have to lose them. And He says that we are blessed when we are poor in heart, and meek, and in mourning. He is saying to His followers, "You are now going to be living on a different plane, a supernatural one, and the rules are different." Just so with the teaching of the Bible on the subject of Satan. It may seem silly and outdated, but use it anyway. You might be surprised.

I have been walking with Jesus for a lot of years now, and while I am still a sinner and have not reached the level of maturity I ought to have reached, I find the Bible's teaching on the supernatural in general, and on Satan in particular, more and more helpful. I used to laugh at demons—until I ran into a demon-possessed man and it scared me to death. I used to say that all healing was psychosomatic until my little girl was made well because people prayed. I used to think that the devil was the "metaphorical personification of evil" until I heard him laughing.

Satan's Work at the Cross

Let's now turn to some of the work of Satan, as it is manifested on the cross of Christ. The Bible teaches that the cross meant more than just a good man dying. On the cross Jesus encountered and defeated all the forces of evil. If you had been standing on Calvary that day, and if you could have had your spiritual blindness removed, you would have seen a cosmic battle taking place. And you would have seen Jesus Christ win the battle.

Jesus was referring to the cross when He told His disciples, "Now judgment is upon this world; now the ruler of this world shall be cast out" (John 12:31). The writer of Hebrews said, "Since then the children share flesh and blood, He Himself likewise also partook of the same, that through death He might render powerless him who had the power of death, that is, the devil" (Heb. 2:14).

I used to wonder why Jesus had to die. Wouldn't it have been better if He had lived His full life? Wouldn't it have been better if He had stayed and taught us? Thirty-three years was simply not enough. When I became a Christian, I understood the necessity of Christ's death for my salvation. And as I have matured in Christ, I have seen more of the nature of Satan and of Christ's victory in His final sacrifice. Let me share with you what I have learned.

Evil's Hatred of Good

It was an existential necessity that Jesus die, because evil cannot stand in the face of good. Peter said in Acts,

> Men of Israel, listen to these words: Jesus the Nazarene, a man attested to you by God with miracles and wonders and signs which God performed through Him in your midst, just as you yourselves know—this man, delivered up by the predetermined plan and foreknowledge of God, you nailed to a cross by the hands of godless men and put Him to death. (Acts 2:22–23)

Again the Scripture says, "For consider Him who has endured such hostility by sinners against Himself" (Heb. 12:3). In Philippians 3:18 we read, "For many walk, of whom I often told you, and now tell you even weeping, that they are enemies of the cross of Christ." There is something about goodness, the goodness of Christ, that required evil to try to destroy it.

In Calvin Miller's *The Singer*, there is a very moving description of the Singer's death. The Singer, you will remember, was the allegorical figure of Jesus; Hater was Satan, and Earth-maker was God. The Singer was being tortured on a great tor-ture machine, and as he died Hater cried out:

"You give me joy and music you will never hear, Singer. Groan for me. Scream the fire that fills your soul. Spew the venom of your grudge upon the city. Never have I known the tri-umph of my hate till now."

He rose and walked across the beam and stepped upon a cable. The added strain drew the manacles into the wrists of the dying Singer.

"Check-mate, Singer!" He howled into the mist and the shrieking of his laughter absorbed into the opaque air.

The Singer felt the agony of dying, the mutilated pain of a hundred thousand men all dying at one time.

With an agility of delight the Hater danced his way around the armature and struggled on the ropes. He looked into the fog again and shouted, "Your move, Earthmaker."

"I have you crying, Earthmaker. You can never glory in your universal riches, for I have made you poor. And there is none to pity you . . .

"You started crying when they broke his hands. Can it be that the agony which plunges you in grief can wash my soul with joy?"[2]

One of the central themes of great literature is the necessary destruction of either evil by good or good by evil. That is one of the themes you will find being played out in Faulkner's Yokna-patawpha County and in the plays of Tennessee Williams. In C. S. Lewis's *Perelandra*, and in the other two books of that tril-ogy, the character named Weston is the personification of evil. When he was not trying to plunge Perelandra into a darkness similar to the darkness of earth, he was destroying beauty. He

2. Calvin Miller, *The Singer*, pp. 123–25.

took magnificently beautiful flowers and crushed them, and he loved to kill small animals with his long fingernails.

A woman once told me that she hated her sister, and in an outburst of anger she cried, "I wish she were dead!" In the silence that followed I asked her why. Speaking through her sobs, she said, "Because she is beautiful and good." Ugliness always seeks the destruction of beauty, and evil seeks the destruction of good.

Anti-Semitism started when the Holy Torah made the Jews different and good. The world doesn't like different and good people, and thus the evil of the world was bent on their destruction. Their righteousness flowing from the law of God was an open invitation to persecution. They were different, and the world's ideal is bland evil. It is a law: evil tries to destroy good.

And so we begin to see something of the necessity of the cross. The absolute goodness and purity of Jesus Christ was an absolute threat to the absolute evil and hatred of Satan. Almost two thousand years have come and gone since Calvary, and things haven't changed much. Evil still tries to destroy good; purity is still the world's proper subject for jokes; honesty is held in derision; and love is washed out in a philosophy of doing your own thing. Just as Satan was behind the cross, so he is behind the destruction of good in our time. When messiahs hang on crosses, and when good men and women do bad, Satan laughs and laughs and laughs.

Evil's Hatred of Truth

There is more instruction to garner from the cross on Calvary. Jesus had to die because a lie cannot stand in the face of truth. In John 1:9–10 we read, "There was the true light which, coming into the world, enlightens every man. He was in the world, and the world was made through Him, and the world did not know Him." Later John wrote, "For the law was given through Moses; grace and truth were realized through Jesus Christ" (1:17). Jesus said to those who tried to kill Him,

But as it is, you are seeking to kill Me, a man who has told you the truth, which I heard from God; this Abraham did not do. You are doing the deeds of your father. . . . You are of your father the devil, and you want to do the desires of your father. He was a murderer from the beginning, and does not stand in the truth, because there is no truth in him. Whenever he speaks a lie, he speaks from his own nature; for he is a liar, and the father of lies. (John 8:40-41, 44)

I was on a radio talk show when a woman called and, as if speaking from Sinai, presented a lie. I called her on it, and do you know what she did? She yelled very loudly and accused me of calling her a liar. When people are caught in lies, they usually grow very angry and defensive. If you have ever been caught in a lie, you know the experience. When that woman became angry at being caught in a lie, she was manifesting one of the operative principles of the universe: a liar unmasked as a liar will hedge, will become angry, and finally will grow destructive. Jesus said, "I am the way, and the truth" (John 14:6), and in that statement we begin to see why He had to die.

One of my daughters brought home a Confederate bill. As we examined it, I was reminded of the time when Jefferson Davis fled from Richmond with three wagons loaded with Confederate money. Davis and the money were captured by Union soldiers, and the Confederate bills were piled up, bale upon bale, in the camp of the Union soldiers. It was cold and windy, and the soldiers were bored and hungry. They decided to play poker with the Confederate money, and they played for a hundred thousand dollars a game. But do you know something? The next morning the soldiers were just as hungry and tired and cold as they had been the night before.

That is the way it is with the world—one great hustle for worthless tender. The point is that Jesus came to tell us so. He was saying, "Look, you're missing the whole reason you were born. That stuff is worthless." He said, "Do not lay up for yourselves treasures upon earth, where moth and rust destroy, and where thieves break in and steal. But lay up for yourselves treasures in heaven, where neither moth nor rust destroys, and where thieves do not break in or steal; for where your treasure is, there will your heart be also" (Matt. 6:19–21).

And Satan looked up from his poker game, took the stogie out of his mouth, focused his eyes on the One who had interrupted the game, pulled out a gun, and shot Him. The Law: a lie will always try to destroy truth. That law still operates, and that is why the men and women of God who bear the truth are persecuted.

It is dangerous, you know, to utter His truth in the world. His truth says that in order to recognize His sovereignty you must give up your own. You either accept it or you kill it. Truth was crucified on Calvary; truth was placed in the tomb; and when that dead Man got up and walked, truth was set loose on the world where no cross would ever stop it again. Jesus had to die because a lie will always seek to destroy the truth, and Satan is the father of lies.

Evil's Hatred of Life

There is one final point you ought to know about the death of Christ on the cross, another law if you will: death will always try to consume and destroy life. Jesus said, "You are of your father the devil, and you want to do the desires of your father. He was a murderer from the beginning" (John 8:44a). In Ephesians 6:12 Satan is called the ruler of darkness, and in Revelation 9:11 he is called the ruler of the abyss. Peter gave this advice: "Be of sober spirit, be on the alert. Your adversary, the devil, prowls about like a roaring lion, seeking someone to devour" (1 Pet. 5:8). The death of Christ on the cross, just because the Son of God was dead, was a source of great delight and joy to the evil one.

Scientists tell us there may be "black holes" in space. They are sometimes called "white dwarfs." A black hole is a star formed in the blink of an eye. As I understand it, the hydrogen fuel of a star burns out, and as the star's core stops burning, gravity pulls the shell inward and crushes all the atoms. I understand that a handful of material from a black hole could weigh

several thousand tons. At any rate, the black hole draws everything into it, including light. Thus, you can't see it in space.

Satan is like that. Everything that is light is sucked into his
sphere to become dark and black. He delights in death, destruction, and darkness. The cross was simply Satan's effort to do
what comes naturally. There the battle between good and evil
reached its climax.

Satan is real, and he is out to get you. That is the bad news.

The Good News of Jesus' Victory

Now let's look at some good news. If you have read the
above and have concluded that the biblical faith is dualistic
(i.e., composed of two equal and opposing forces, one good and
one evil), you have made a terrible mistake. Nothing could be
farther from the truth.

The Bible teaches that there *are* two forces, one good and one
evil; however, it does not teach that the two forces are equal.
The Bible teaches that God is sovereign over everything and
that Satan's existence is only tolerated because he fits into the
economy of God. In the book of Job, there is an interesting
dialogue between God and Satan.

Now there was a day when the sons of God came to present
themselves before the Lord, Satan also came among them. And
the Lord said to Satan, "From where do you come?" Then Satan
answered the Lord and said, "From roaming about on the earth
and walking around on it." And the Lord said to Satan, "Have
you considered My servant Job? For there is no one like him on
the earth, a blameless and upright man, fearing God and turning
away from evil." Then Satan answered the Lord, "Does Job fear
God for nothing? Hast Thou not made a hedge about him and his
house and all that he has, on every side? Thou hast blessed the
work of his hands, and his possessions have increased in the land.
But put forth Thy hand now and touch all that he has; he will
surely curse Thee to Thy face." Then the Lord said to Satan,
"Behold, all that he has is in your power, only do not put forth
your hand on him." So Satan departed from the presence of the
Lord. (Job 1:6–12)

There are several interesting things about that passage, but the most important is that Satan had to ask God's permission before going after Job. In other words, Satan is God's lackey acting only with God's permission.

The Westminster catechisms say the chief end of man is "to glorify God and to enjoy Him forever." Did you ever think that glorifying God is totally unnecessary? As a matter of fact, *everything will* glorify God either the easy way or the hard way. The Scripture says, "Therefore also God highly exalted Him [Christ], and bestowed on Him the name which is above every name, that at the name of Jesus every knee should bow, of those who are in heaven, and on earth, and under the earth, and that every tongue should confess that Jesus Christ is Lord, to the glory of God the Father" (Phil. 2:9–11). The Christian faith is not dualistic. Everything that was created was created for one purpose, to glorify God. As a matter of fact, even Satan will glorify God.

That is part of the good news, but there is more: the Christian is playing in a ball game that has been fixed. The contest has already been decided! The victory has already been won! Satan will come out on the short end of the stick! You can count on it because on the cross of Christ Satan's end was secured, and in the empty tomb the believer's victory was made manifest. The Scripture says,

> Since the children have flesh and blood, he too shared in their humanity so that by his death he might destroy him who holds the power of death—that is, the devil—and free those who all their lives were held in slavery by their fear of death.... For this reason he had to be made like his brothers in every way, in order that he might become a merciful and faithful high priest in service to God, and that he might make atonement for the sins of the people. Because he himself suffered when he was tempted, he is able to help those who are being tempted. (Heb. 2:14–15, 17–18 NIV)

The fact of Satan's defeat, however, should not lull the Christian into believing the devil is powerless. Martin Luther told his followers they ought to be very careful of Satan because he had years of experience on them. If the battle is to be won, it must be won by Christ in our lives, not by our power to resist and fight.

Dealing with Satan

Very quickly, let me give you some practical helps for dealing with Satan. God has given us the gift of prayer in the name of Christ, and that gift ought to be utilized. When Jesus taught His disciples to pray, He told them to pray to be delivered from "the evil one" (see Matt. 6:13 NKJV, where a proper translation of the traditional "evil" ought to be the personal, "evil one"), and when Jesus was warning Peter, He said, "Simon, Simon, behold, Satan has demanded permission to sift you like wheat; but I have prayed for you, that your faith may not fail; and you, when once you have turned again, strengthen your brothers" (Luke 22:31–32). When you are overwhelmed by temptation, burdened with the evil within your own heart and from others, depressed beyond the help of modern pop psychology, try praying in the name of Christ that Satan be banished. It is a powerful prayer.

The second tool God has given the Christian to appropriate the victory already won is faith. In the sixth chapter of Ephesians, Paul gave the Christian a list of weapons to use when doing battle with Satan, "...in addition to all, taking up the shield of faith with which you will be able to extinguish all the flaming missiles of the evil one" (Eph. 6:16). Another word for faith is *trust*. Paul was saying that the Christian ought to be developing (and it is a process) a walk with Christ that enables him to trust or have faith in His ability to deal with all that Satan can do to the Christian. In the movie *My Bodyguard*, a boy was being intimidated by the bullies at his high school. He talked one big, mean kid into being his bodyguard, and thereafter he was able to stand up to all the intimidation. You have a Bodyguard, and only a fool will wander far from Him.

Third, the Christian aids in the appropriation of Christ's victory over Satan with watchfulness. Peter said, "Be of sober spirit, be on the alert. Your adversary, the devil, prowls about like a roaring lion" (1 Pet. 5:8). Don't assume you are too spiritual to be attacked by the tempter; nobody is. Don't think that because you have read your Bible and prayed you are free from the possibility of evil; nobody is. Don't think there is some magic formula that will exempt you from the devil's plans; there isn't. The closer you draw to Jesus, the closer Satan will try to draw to you. If you know that, you will be watchful. After almost every spiritual victory in your life you will be open to depression, doubt, pride, anger, and evil thoughts. Someone has said, "If you didn't meet Satan this morning, it's a pretty good indication you were going in the same direction." To be forewarned is to be forearmed!

Fourth, in order to appropriate the victory won for you on the cross, be feisty in your resistance. The Bible says, "But resist him [Satan], firm in your faith" (1 Pet. 5:9a). James said, "Resist the devil and he will flee from you" (James 4:7b). It's dangerous to believe that if you do nothing, everything will be okay. God didn't design the world that way, and He didn't design you that way. You were meant to be active in your walk with Christ.

Now, please notice that I didn't tell you to fight the battle yourself or insist that your heroic effort will defeat Satan. That isn't what the Scriptures mean when they talk about resistance. The passage I quoted from James has two parts: "Submit therefore to God. [then] Resist the devil and he will flee from you." Satan knows you belong to Christ and that you stand with His hedge about you: so he flees.

Do you remember in *The Wizard of Oz* when Dorothy, the lion, the tin man, and the scarecrow finally reached the Wizard? The Wizard was an awe-inspiring figure frightening everyone except, of course, Toto, Dorothy's little dog. Toto ran to the curtain and pulled it back, revealing a little man pulling the levers that controlled the gigantic, fake wizard. Satan is sort of like that wizard. If you check him out in the power of Christ, if you resist him, you will find that he isn't as big as you thought. There is an old English proverb that says, "Fear knocked at the door, faith answered, and no one was there." Apply that proverb to Satan and it fits: Satan knocked at the door, faith answered, and no one was there.

Truth is a strong weapon against Satan. In the Ephesians passage I quoted, Paul said, "Stand firm therefore, having girded your loins with truth." Again, "And take the helmet of salvation, and the sword of the Spirit, which is the word of God" (Eph. 6:14, 17). The best way to deal with the "father of lies" is to apply a heavy dose of truth. Satan will tell you that you are powerless against him; he will say you don't belong to Christ; he will make you afraid and tell you the Bible isn't true. When that happens, speak the truth, "When He [God] had disarmed the rulers and authorities, He made a public display of them, having triumphed over them through Him [Christ]" (Col. 2:15). That is a fact, and you can stand on it.

I remember one time when I was visiting a small church in the Philippines. The church was nestled back in the mountains, and when we made the long journey to worship at the church, I really didn't expect to find very many people or a very exciting ministry. When we drove up to the church, however, it was difficult to get past the large crowd of people standing in the streets trying to get into the small church building.

After the service I asked the young pastor about the great and excited crowd. He told me that two weeks before there had been a woman in their village who through involvement with the occult had become possessed by a demon. Everything had been tried to help her. The local witch doctor had been called, and he had spent days trying to deal with the satanic power possessing her. The woman's family was frantic and had no one else to turn to but the pastor and his elders. He told me they had gone in the power of Christ and had rebuked Satan and prayed for the woman. The people of the village had started coming to the church in droves because they had seen the power of God.

I asked him what happened when he went to see the woman. I will never forget his answer: "Jesus won. Satan lost."

7   A HERITAGE OF LOVE

If Jesus has come . . .
love will last.

I am convinced that neither death, nor life, nor angels, nor principali-
ties, nor things present, nor things to come, nor powers, nor height, nor
depth, nor any other created thing, shall be able to separate us from the love
of God, which is in Christ Jesus our Lord.

Romans 8:38–39

There is an old story about a man who dreamed he was given a tour of heaven and hell. In hell he saw a very long table that stretched for miles. On the table he saw platters of the most delicious food he had ever seen. Thousands upon thousands of people, as far as he could see, were sitting on both sides of the table. When he examined the scene more closely, he noticed that the people sitting at the table were not getting much to eat because they were required by the proprietor of the establishment to eat with four-foot-long spoons. You can imagine how difficult that would be; you would be able to get the food on the spoon, but to get it into your mouth would be difficult if not impossible. The man noticed the people were angry at one another, withdrawn, and bitter. But more than that, he noticed the people in hell were hungry.

Much to his astonishment, the man saw the same scene in heaven: the long table, the delicious food, and the four-foot-long spoons. But in heaven the people were happy and well-fed. He tried to see the difference between the scene in heaven and the one in hell, and he discovered that the only difference was that in heaven the people were feeding each other across the table.

That is a good story, and it certainly has a lot of truth in it, but the question before the house is this: does the story really tell the whole truth? In other words, could it be that it is just a nice story and doesn't reflect the way the world really works? Will people ever love each other and work together that well, even in heaven?

In the last chapter we saw that one of life's universal principles is that it is the nature of hate to destroy love. In his superb book *Reflections of a Neoconservative*, Irving Kristol titled an essay, "Machiavelli and the Profanation of Politics." In his essay, he delineated the harsh and "practical" views of Machiavellianism in regard to power politics divorced from any arbitrary moral system. At the close of the essay, Kristol wrote,

> There have been three major figures in the history of Western thought during the last five centuries who have rejected Christianity, not for its failure to live up to its values, but because they repudiated these values themselves. The three are Machiavelli, de Sade, and Nietzsche. A great part of the intellectual history of the modern era can be told in terms of the efforts of a civilization still Christian, to come to terms with Machiavelli in politics, de Sade in sex, Nietzsche in philosophy. These efforts have been ingenious, but hardly successful. The "save morality"of Christianity is constantly in retreat before the revolt of "the masters," with every new *modus vivendi* an unstable armistice. Heidegger has even gone so far as to say that the struggle is over—that with Nietzsche the Christian epoch draws to a close. If this is so, then it can also be said that Machiavelli marks the beginning of this end.[1]

Paul said there are three things that will last forever, faith, hope, and love, and then he said that the greatest of the three is love (see 1 Cor. 13:13). But is that really true? Do you ever wonder if Christians haven't chosen the losing side? Do you ever look around, see the prosperity and success of those who

1. Irving Kristol, *Reflections of a Neoconservative* (New York: Basic Books, 1983), pp. 134–35.

have divorced themselves from love, and wonder if maybe they are right? Is love really better than hate?

Those are fair questions, and the Bible is not afraid to pose them honestly:

> For I was envious of the arrogant,
> As I saw the prosperity of the wicked.
> For there are no pains in their death;
> And their body is fat.
> They are not in trouble as other men;
> Nor are they plagued like mankind.
> Therefore pride is their necklace;
> The garment of violence covers them.
> Their eye bulges from fatness;
> The imaginations of their heart run riot.
> They mock, and wickedly speak of oppression;
> They speak from on high.
> They have set their mouth against the heavens,
> And their tongue parades through the earth....
> And they say, "How does God know?
> And is there knowledge with the Most High?"
> Behold, these are the wicked;
> And always at ease, they have increased in wealth.
> Surely in vain I have kept my heart pure,
> And washed my hands in innocence;
> For I have been stricken all day long,
> And chastened every morning. (Ps. 73:3-9, 11-13)

In Albert Camus's play *Cross Purposes*, a mother and her daughter rob and murder a boarder staying at their inn. To their horror, they discover the man is really the husband of the mother and the father of the daughter. Maria is then hated by her daughter Martha, who decides she will commit suicide. She says to her mother:

> We did to your husband last night what we had done to other travellers before; we killed him and took his money.... If you must know, there was a misunderstanding. And if you have any experience at all of the world, that won't surprise you.... Your tears revolt me.... But fix this in your mind; neither for him nor for us, neither in life nor in death, is there any peace or homeland. For you'll agree one can hardly call it a home, that place of clotted

darkness underground, to which we go from here, to feed blind animals....We're cheated, I tell you. Cheated! What do they serve, those blind impulses that surge up in us, the yearnings that rack our souls? Why cry out for the sea, or for love? What futility! Your husband knows now what the answer is: that charnel house where in the end we shall lie huddled together, side by side....Try to realize that no grief of yours can ever equal the injustice done to man.[2]

I move the previous question: is love really stronger than hate? The question prompts many more. When the last page of history has been turned, will the hero be Jesus or Hitler? If we have enemies, is it better to love them or to hate them? We live in a dog-eat-dog world: should we really even consider the way of love? Isn't love the way of weakness? Those are the questions posed by this chapter.

The Bible's answer is clear: God is love, and God rules the universe. Because He is love and is sovereign, the final outcome of love will be victory. The Bible says that the best way to deal with people is to love them—even our enemies. We are promised that in the end love will destroy hate. That all sounds good, but we weren't sure it was true until Jesus came. Because Jesus has come, love has conquered because *He* has conquered.

Jesus, the Proof of Love's Conquest

Jesus is God's key to *knowing* that love is stronger than hate. Let me illustrate what I mean. Perhaps you remember when the University of Miami won the national football championship. Those of us who live in Miami will never forget it. For years the UM football team had received very little attention. When we finally had the best football team in the nation, nobody could believe it. But we knew they were the best. We knew that Howard Schnellenberger was the best football coach in the nation and that nobody was going to beat the University of Miami.

Of course our "knowing" could have been attributed to

2. Quoted in Vincent Miceli, *The Gods of Atheism* (New Rochelle, N.Y.: Arlington House, 1971), pp. 200–201.

wishful thinking, partisan football fever, or hometown hopes. But when Miami received its invitation to the Orange Bowl against the football giants of Nebraska, we had a chance to check out our knowing. And when the University of Miami emerged victorious, our knowing was affirmed by everybody else in the nation.

Before that Orange Bowl, UM was the best in the nation. The Orange Bowl did not change the reality; it just confirmed it. In other words, Miami won at the Orange Bowl because they *were* the best; they didn't win at the Orange Bowl and thus *become* the best.

That is a good illustration of what happened when Jesus was victorious. (Please, for those of you who are partisan football fans, don't miss the point because you happen to believe that UM was not the best that year.) For years, the believers knew that love was better than hate. Those who knew God knew that He was love and that His ultimate victory was assured. But in Christ their knowing was affirmed. The reality of love's victory was made clear. That is what John meant when he wrote, "Beloved, I am not writing a new commandment to you, but an old commandment which you have had from the beginning; the old commandment is the word which you have heard. On the other hand, I am writing a new commandment to you, which is true in Him and in you, because the darkness is passing away, and the true light is already shining" (1 John 2:7-8). Again John wrote,

> Beloved, let us love one another, for love is from God; and every one who loves is born of God and knows God. The one who does not love does not know God, for God is love. [That sounds good, but how do we know?] By this the love of God was manifested in us, that God has sent His only begotten Son into the world so that we might live through Him. (1 John 4:7-9)

The story of Christmas is a love story. Don't be confused by the trinkets and the glitter. It's not even about babies, stables, and wise men. Christmas is about love. "For God so loved the

world, that He gave His only begotten Son" (John 3:16a).
Love came down at Christmas.

The Vocabulary of Love

Have you ever noticed the way God relates to the world? He
never dreams up a new vocabulary. He uses the one we use. He
never communicates in a category that is unrelated to human
experience; rather, He communicates through it. For instance,
take the sacrament of the Lord's Supper. It was no accident that
Jesus used bread and wine; common things like bread and wine
are a part of the relational vocabulary of God to His people. In
the twenty-third psalm, God related to His people with green
pastures, still waters, and death. He spoke to us in our own
terms. That is why Calvin called the Bible "God's baby talk."
When you think about God and all His power and greatness,
the fact that He relates to us at all is amazing; but the fact that
He relates with a language we can understand is absolutely astounding.

Love is no exception. Love is universal. Do you remember
the first time you fell in love? Of course it was puppy love, but it
was, nevertheless, real to the puppy. Your only interest had
been cowboys and Indians and mud pies until you discovered
that special boy or girl.

In our congregation there is a young man who decided on a
unique way to propose to his beloved. His name is Steve Vensel,
and Steve never does anything in a bland way. He had some
friends invite his sweetheart, Dory, to a picnic in a public park.
What she didn't know was that he had dressed as a knight in
shining armor, had rented a horse, and was waiting in the trees
off to the side of the park. When Dory was settled down for the
picnic, he approached her on his horse, climbed down, and
knelt before her. This is what he said: "Fair Princess, I have
searched for thee. I have journeyed far and long in my quest,
and many sorrows have I known. Yet in vain has not my quest
been, for who doth cause my heart to sing but the King Himself. And my heart sings for thee. I am but a knight in the ser-

vice of the Prince. Riches of gold and silver and jewels I cannot give. But that which is most precious have I guarded for this day. My heart, my love, my very life have I reserved for thee. These are the gifts I offer.... Alas, Princess, it is thee I love. It is with thee I wish to endeavor life's journey. Wouldst thou take my hand in marriage? Wouldst thou ride with me and me alone?" Needless to say, Dory accepted his proposal.

When we talk about love, we can all understand it to one degree or another because we have all been in love. And it is no accident that the relationship between God and His creation is also one of love. Listen to some of the Scriptures relating to the way God loves: "Indeed, He loves the people; all Thy holy ones are in Thy hand, and they followed in Thy steps" (Deut. 33:3). "Just as a father has compassion on his children, so the Lord has compassion on those who fear Him" (Ps. 63:3). "I have loved you with an everlasting love" (Jer. 31:3). God relates to us in the language of love, a language we can understand.

In order to understand the kind of love about which the Scripture speaks, it is important that we stop for a moment and define it. We live in a culture that mimics the real love manifested in the Bible: "What the world needs now is love, sweet love." "Lay a little love on me, baby." It's been said so often that I hesitate to say it again, but I will: the Greeks had a number of different words that we translate into our English word *love*. One of their words meant to love someone sexually, another to love someone as a brother, another to like someone, and still another to like some*thing*. But the best Greek word, and the one used to describe God's love, was the word *agape. Agape* love is that kind of determined love that wills and does the best for someone regardless of his response.

Some things can be defined in terms of what they are, but others can only be defined in terms of what they do. Love is of the latter. Love, in order to be love, must express itself. The Bible says that God is love; and if that is true, His love must find a tangible expression. That is what the incarnation is all about.

God's "Problems" in Loving Us

Have you ever considered the fact that God has a problem with His love? We can identify with His problem because we all have had the experience of trying to relate to someone who didn't even know he was being loved. Again, God communicates to us in the language and the experience we understand so we can, with as little presumption as possible, understand His problem. He was faced with a number of questions. Let's check them out.

The first question is this: what do you do if you love someone and the person you love doesn't even know you exist? Of course, you can try to get that person to notice you. I can remember the first time I was in love. I had no idea in the world how to meet this special girl until I saw her in a drugstore standing near the soda fountain. I decided it was my one chance; so I bought two milk shakes and took one to her. But she didn't want a milk shake. Furthermore, she thought I was an arrogant stranger trying to bring her one without asking. She turned and walked away, leaving me standing there with two milk shakes in my hands. I decided I didn't want a milk shake, either. You must be very careful when you want to love someone who doesn't even know you exist.

Perhaps the best way to get the person you love to notice you is to get someone to introduce you. In the church I serve, I am often asked by a young man or woman to make an introduction to someone he or she has seen across the church. (One of the great joys I have is to make an introduction, see the couple grow together, get married, and produce little Presbyterians.)

Remember that God relates to us with an experience that is similar to our own. The prophets were the introducers. The God of the universe, the God of Abraham, Isaac, and Jacob, was doing no more and no less than sending messages through them to a people He loved.

Eternity in Their Hearts is a fascinating book by Don Richardson that shows how cultures have been prepared for hearing the gospel. In every culture, in every place, God has planted the seeds of His love by revealing Himself in various ways. For example, I grew up in the mountains of North Carolina near the Cherokee Indian reservation. Recently, on a visit home, my wife and I attended a lecture on Cherokee theology, and we were astounded. The Indians of North Carolina had a theological system so sophisticated that it is difficult to understand where they got it. Before the missionaries ever came to the Cherokee, they believed there was one God and that He manifested Himself in three Persons. They believed idolatry was wrong and that the God they worshiped was a loving God. I believe God was preparing a culture for the manifestation of His love.

It is an old movie plot, and it has been used over and over again. The woman is either a minor actress in a play or a dancer in a musical. She has a secret admirer in the audience every night. Night after night, she receives a dozen roses with no name attached, just a card that reads, "From a secret admirer." She begins to wonder who he could be; she dreams of what he will look like; she thinks of him often. And then finally he asks her to dinner, and they fall in love and live happily ever after.

That is what God has done. We didn't know Him, but He knew us and loved us. He sent roses; sometimes the roses were the prophets, at other times a gentle push of a cultural idea. Sometimes He whispered His love in the trees and the sunsets. And then at Christmas, God signed the card.

I read the other day of a clergyman who counsels engaged couples. He said that when he asks a couple how long they've known each other, almost without exception the woman will say three or four years and the man will say two or three years. He drew the following conclusions: the man didn't even know the woman existed for a whole year. She knew him and loved him even before he knew she existed. Likewise, God knew us and loved us even before we knew He existed. John said, "In this is love, not that we loved God, but that He loved us and sent His Son to be the propitiation for our sins....We love, because He first loved us" (1 John 4:10, 19).

There is a second question: what do you do if you love someone and the person you love doesn't love you back? Unrequited love is a horrible thing, and the interesting thing about it is that the people who suffer from it almost always do the wrong thing. They manipulate: "I have cancer, and I only have a short time to live. Couldn't you find it in your heart to give me a little time?" They use force: "I know you don't love me, but if you don't learn to, I'll beat up your little brother." They use persistence: "You have no choice. I am going to pressure you and pursue you until you give up." They use guilt: "I have loved you for so long; I have taken you places; I have stood with you and defended you. The least you could do is love me a little. If you don't, I'll kill myself and you'll be sorry."

There is a young woman in Sicily who is not interested in the affections of her persistent suitor. But he keeps on pressing the matter. His name is Stefano Cambria, and her name is Maria Barbieri. After trying to discourage Stefano as much as possible, she finally called the police and had a restraining order issued against him. He was prevented from seeing her or talking to her on the phone on penalty of going to jail. Of course, a restraining order was not enough to keep Stefano from Maria, and he was thrown in jail. Every time he gets out of jail, he goes to the nearest phone and calls Maria. At the last count, Stefano has been in jail eleven times. When someone doesn't love you, it can be a horrible thing.

God is wise in the ways of love. He knows that if you want to get someone to love you back, you have to learn to be gentle. You catch a loved one the same way you catch a mountain trout. You do it very carefully and very gently. That, dear reader, is what God did at Christmas. He knew that loves takes a while. He knew us. And so He whispered. That is why He came as a baby instead of as a king.

I have a German shepherd named Calvin. He came to us one night almost by accident. Someone had beaten him and intimidated him, and when Calvin wouldn't respond, he was set loose on the island where we lived. He showed up at our house at three in the morning, and he never left. When Calvin first came to us, he was afraid of men because, I suppose, he had been beaten by a man. He related quite well to my daughters and my wife, but not to me. I tried everything to get him to come to me. I tried feeding him, and petting him, and talking softly to him, but nothing seemed to work. After a few months, however, I got the feeling he was deciding I wasn't going to hurt him. Some evenings I would be reading the paper, and I would feel a soft nudge at my elbow. I would turn around to see Calvin running in the opposite direction. I gave it time, and little by little, Calvin and I have become friends. I learned that in order to get Calvin to return my love, I had to be very gentle and patient.

To a much greater degree, God expressed His love in a gentle and patient way. "And this will be a sign for you; you will find a baby wrapped in cloths, and lying in a manger" (Luke 2:12).

A third question is this: what do you do if you love someone and the person you love is not worthy of your love? A young man told me not too long ago that he had given up dating. I asked him if he were shy, and he said that wasn't his problem. He said, "The problem is that I can't find a woman who will please Mother." In other words, his mother had decided no woman was good enough for her son. The Father God decided that, too. The only difference between God and the mother is that she was wrong in her opinion and God hit the nail on the head.

One of the problems with "celebrity Christianity" is that people begin to get the idea that God only loves those who are attractive: if you are beautiful, charming, or athletic, then God will love you. Let me tell you something: there are no attractive people as far as God's holiness is concerned. When you measure beauty, charm, and athletic prowess by perfection, there is no such thing as beauty, charm, or athletic prowess. How much truer is this if you measure human goodness by perfection? You have to cry out with the prophet, "The heart is more deceitful than all else and is desperately sick; who can understand it?" (Jer. 17:9).

This summer, both my daughters are in other countries on mission projects. My elder daughter, Robin, is in Europe witnessing in youth hostels in a number of countries, and Jennifer is in the Dominican Republic helping build churches in the poor areas of the country. I want you to know that I have been terribly worried about them both. I know how I *ought* to feel. I ought to be proud that they are sharing their faith in Christ with people who have never heard of His love, and I suppose I have a lot of that pride. I ought to be glad that my daughters love God enough to go to a sinful world, and I guess I really am. But mostly I am worried, and sometimes I think, "There isn't a sinner in the world who is worth either one of my daughters." Those were the thoughts I had the other day, and I was telling the Father about them. But then He reminded me that if He had felt that way, I would never have known His love. He reminded me again that He loved the world, that He gave His only Son, and that nobody in the world was worthy of that gift.

I read the other day of a teenager who bought his girlfriend an orchid. It was the first orchid he had ever bought and the first one she had ever received. There was a card with the orchid, and it read, "With all my love, and most of my allowance." Well, God said, "With all of my love, and all of my allowance. I love you this much."

What do you do when the one you love is not worthy of your love? You don't stop loving, because worth is not a factor in love. Hosea learned that when he was commanded by God to marry the prostitute Gomer. God said to Hosea that that was what love was all about. You don't explain love; who knows why a princess loves an ugly frog? She just does. God loved us when we didn't deserve it, and that is what the incarnation is all about.

Finally, what do you do if you love someone who is *never* going to love you back? You've heard the saying, "When you love something, set it free, and if it never returns to you, it was never meant to be." There is something insipid about that, but there is some truth to it, too. Love that is forced is not love. It is manipulation.

I can force my family to show the signs of love, but I can't force them to love me even though I am bigger and stronger than they are. I can say to my daughters, "You love me or I will never speak to you again." I can say to them, "I will hit you and hurt you if you don't love me." Then they will hug me and kiss me and do nice things for me, but they will never love me. Do you know why? Because love, in order to be love, must have a choice.

The incarnation was the time when the God of the universe put the ball into the court of the world. He said: "I love you. I have demonstrated My love, but I will not force it on you. You must come to Me yourself. You don't have to come with a gift, or with purity, or with a love like Mine. But you must come. If you are thirsty, I will give you living water because I love you. But you must drink. If you are hungry, I will give you the bread of life because I love you. But you must eat. If you are tired and weary, I will give you rest because I love you. But you must lean on Me. If you are sinful and dirty, I will forgive you and clean you up because I love you. But you must come."

This is the dark side of the incarnation. If Jesus has come, love has conquered hate: but there will be those who will never know love's victory. They have placed themselves on the wrong side of the battlefield.

The Absolutes of Love

Let's look at the four absolutes of love in the remainder of this chapter. First, God is love (see 1 John 4:8). God doesn't just love; He doesn't just act in a loving way; He doesn't just do loving things. He *is* love. If He is love, everything that flows from His being is loving. The world is a manifestation of His love; all creation points to the power of His love. The hymnist Frederick Faber put it very well:

> For the love of God is broader
> Than the measure of man's mind,
> And the heart of the Eternal
> Is most wonderfully kind.

You don't have to plead with the sun to shine, nor do you

have to hope that water is wet. It is stupid to pray that fire will burn or that an apple will have seeds. The wetness of water, the shining of the sun, the burning of fire, and the seeds of apples are all the attributes of those things. Just so, love is an attribute of God. He is love.

The second absolute is this: Jesus is the perfect manifestation of the attribute of God's love. Jesus said, "Just as the Father has loved Me, I have also loved you; abide in My love" (John 15:9). Commenting on the incarnation, John said, "The Father loves the Son, and has given all things into His hand" (John 3:35). And in his first letter, John said, "By this the love of God was manifested in us, that God has sent His only begotten Son into the world so that we might live through Him" (1 John 4:9).

It was World War II, and the battle was fierce. Jerry had been wounded and was dying in a no man's land. Jerry's buddy pleaded with his sergeant to be able to go to his friend's aid. At first the sergeant refused. He said, "Are you crazy? You'll be killed, too. There isn't anything you or anyone else can do." But Jim persisted, and finally the sergeant relented and allowed him to go. Jim made his way under the barbed wire and through the mud and slush. Two hours later he came back carrying the body of his dead friend. The sergeant said, "See, I told you it wasn't worth it. He's dead."

"No sir," replied the soldier, "it was worth it. When I got to him he was still alive, and he said, 'Jim, I knew you would come.' "

That is real love because love will always act. Jesus is the loving action of God. The difference between Jim's trip into no man's land and Jesus' trip into no man's land is not in the love. The love was the same. The difference between Jim and Jesus is that Jesus brought us back alive.

The third absolute is that the Holy Spirit creates the same love in us that is an attribute of God and is manifested in Jesus. Romans 5:5 says, "The love of God has been poured out within our hearts through the Holy Spirit who was given to us."

You can't manufacture love! The materials are simply not available. They are only sold in one place, and that is the store owned and operated by the Holy Spirit. To those who have turned to Christ and His manifestation of love on the cross, the Holy Spirit gives a gift far more important than teaching, prophecy, tongues, knowledge, healing, wisdom, or faith. The Holy Spirit gives God's people love.

Love is not natural to human beings. It has been said that you have to be taught to hate. That's a lie. You don't have to be taught to hate. Hate comes naturally. Watch children at play and take particular note of their essential cruelty toward one another. Watch adults at play, and you will see the same cruelty, only hidden better. Racism, war, and selfishness are reflections of normal humanity. Thomas Brown's little ditty is our experience:

> I do not love thee, Dr. Fell;
> The reason why I cannot tell;
> But this I know, and know full well:
> I do not love thee, Dr. Fell.

My dear friend Ara Tchividjian lived as an Armenian boy in Turkey during the Armenian genocide. The Turks said they would protect the Tchividjian family if they would deny their faith. They refused. Then the Turks said that if they would not talk about their faith they would be protected. They accepted their protection—which was short-lived. The Turkish soldiers surrounded the Tchividjian home. But the sounds of their compatriots dying was too much too bear, and Mrs. Tchividjian escaped her protectors, and her son Ara eventually ended up in Switzerland. Ara Tchividjian's oldest son is Stephan, and when Stephan was old enough to understand, his father gave him a gun and said, "Son, if you ever meet those who killed your grandfather, you will kill them. If you do not kill them, you are no longer my son."

Some years later Ara Tchividjian became a Christian. On the day he encountered the love of Christ, he went to Stephan and asked for the gun. He told his son, "If I ever meet those who killed your grandfather, I will throw my arms around them and tell them that I love them." Where did he get that kind of love? I'll tell you. He got it from the Spirit of God, the God who is love and who has manifested that love in His Son.

There is one final absolute: not only is the first person of the Trinity, God the Father, love; not only is the second person of the Trinity, God the Son, the manifestation of love; not only is the third person of the Trinity, God the Holy Spirit, the creator of love; but the church, the focal point of the Trinity's love, is effective and powerful because of love. In the great hymn of love in 1 Corinthians 13, Paul said,

> If I speak with the tongues of men and of angels, but do not have love, I have become a noisy gong or a clanging cymbal. And if I have the gift of prophecy, and know all mysteries and all knowledge; and if I have all faith, so as to remove mountains, but do not have love, I am nothing. And if I give all my possessions to feed the poor, and if I deliver my body to be burned, but do not have love, it profits me nothing....But now abide faith, hope, love, these three; but the greatest of these is love. (1 Cor. 13:1-3, 13)

What is God saying in this chapter? It is an astounding revelation. He is saying, "I don't care who you are, what you do, how much you have, how great your gifts are, or how much you know; if you don't have love, you are a clanging cymbal, useless for anything except making noise."

When all is said and done, hate will be destroyed. You see, hate can only exist in opposition to love. It is not something that exists in its own right. Love, white-hot love, will burn up everything that is not love. The road of hate is the road of ultimate destruction. How do I know? Because a dead man got up and walked, and when He got out of the grave, the love of the Father that He manifested was let loose on the world, where it will never be destroyed—ever.

Perhaps the greatest teacher of love as manifested in Jesus was the apostle John. He was the writer of the gospel and letters that bear his name. Running throughout both the gospel of John and his letters is the theme of love. Tradition says that John was commanded to deny Christ by the Roman proconsul in Ephesus in accordance with an edict from the emperor. It is said that John replied, "It behooves us to obey God more than man. Hence I will neither deny Christ nor desist from preaching His name, but will continue the course of my ministry which I received from the Lord."[3] At this reply the proconsul tortured John and finally exiled him to the island of Patmos.

If ever there was a man who had reason to hate, harbor bitterness, or be angry, it was the apostle John. It is said, however, that he never lost the love Christ had given him. He returned to his beloved Ephesus during the last days of his life, and tradition says that on the day of his death, he was carried by his friends on a pallet to the church assembly where he had served so long and faithfully as their pastor. The congregation asked him to speak to them one more time. He made one comment: "Love one another."

The people in the congregation asked John why he always said this, and he replied: "Because there is nothing else!"[4]

That's it. If Jesus has come, love really has conquered.

3. Emil G. Kraeling, *The Disciples* (Chicago: Rand McNally & Company, 1966), p. 149.
4. H. S. Vigeveno, *Thirteen Men Who Changed the World* (Glendale: Regal Books, 1967), p. 126.

8   A HERITAGE OF IMMORTALITY

If Jesus has come...
death has died.

Christ Jesus... abolished death, and brought life and immortality to light through the gospel.

2 Timothy 1:10

One of the most fascinating occurrences of our time is the scientific interest generated by the Shroud of Turin. Many believe it is the shroud in which the corpse of Jesus was wrapped before His resurrection. The shroud's history is complex, and many details are obscure. Its existence was not generally known until 1357, when it was exhibited in the French provincial town of Lirey.

In 1898, Secondo Pia was allowed to photograph the shroud for the first time. To his astonishment, when he looked at the negatives of his pictures, he found they presented a highly detailed picture of a man who had been crucified.

The next showing of the shroud took place in 1931, when detailed photographs were taken by Giuseppe Enrie. The photographs he took that year became the basis of study by physicians and scientists in France, England, Italy, Germany, and the United States. Their conclusions were not unanimous in every detail, but they all agreed on one matter: the imprints in the shroud are those of a human corpse in a pronounced state of rigor mortis.

In 1978, there was a major development in the study of the shroud. A team of scientists, known as the Shroud of Turin Research Project, converged on Turin, Italy. The Catholic church had allowed an object of faith to be inspected with the neutral analytical tools of modern science, and it was an opportunity not to be missed. Dozens of scientists of every religious belief and unbelief were invited to examine the shroud to settle once and for all its authenticity. It was the most thorough examination of a religious relic by the scientific community in history. Millions of dollars in sophisticated testing equipment was taken to the Renaissance reception room in the royal palace of the House of Savoy. For five days, the most rigorous and detailed testing of the shroud took place. Then the results were tested and retested in the laboratories of scientists in Europe and the United States. The preliminary results are nothing less than astounding.

First, the shroud and the image on it are not counterfeit. The shroud contained a corpse of a crucified man about five feet ten inches tall. The facial expression is peaceful, especially compared to the tortured and punctured body.

Second, the anatomy pictured on the shroud shows details that weren't even known until the eighteenth century. In other words, an artist would have had to travel six hundred years into the future to learn the information necessary to produce a counterfeit.

Third, there are actual blood stains on the fourteen-foot shroud. There is also an amazing accuracy in terms of blood flow and consistency. The corpse in the shroud died with nails through the upper part of his hands, and a nail was driven through his feet. The blood stains show there was a crown of thorns or a similar object on his forehead. There was a lance wound in his side.

Fourth, pollen discovered in the threads of the shroud has been shown to be from first-century Palestine.

Fifth, there has been a computer enhancement of the image on the shroud that makes the image three–dimensional. That image is especially interesting, because it shows that coins were placed over the eyes of the corpse. The coins bear an amazing resemblance to those issued by Pontius Pilate in the years A.D. 31–34.

Sixth, the back of the shroud shows small lash marks. The details of these wounds are amazing in that they show exactly the marks that would have been left by a Roman flagrum, an instrument of torture used much like a whip.

I could go on and on.[1]

By far, the most interesting mystery about the Shroud of Turin is how the corpse got out of the shroud. The facts militate against the body's being removed from the shroud by any human means, because the blood stains have not been smudged. Further, the body in the shroud did not decompose while wrapped in it. Pathologists are the sure the man was dead, but the scientific tests found no evidence of decomposition beyond the initial signs of death. That, of course, indicates the body was in the shroud for a very short period.

The scientific tests suggest the image on the shroud was caused by a very intense and momentary blast of heat and light, much like radiation. It has been impossible for scientists to duplicate the image. Dr. Bucklin, the deputy medical examiner for Los Angeles County said, "The medical data from the Shroud supports the resurrection. When this medical information is combined with the physical, chemical, and historical facts, there is strong evidence for Jesus' resurrection." The medical facts have convinced Dr. Bucklin that the Shroud of Turin is the burial cloth of Jesus Christ.[2]

Did the Shroud of Turin contain the body of Jesus? Maybe. However, the reaction of many to the scientific data surrounding the shroud is more fascinating than the data itself. Rarely has opposition to a scientific investigation been so shrill. When the facts began to indicate Jesus was the body in the shroud,

---

1. Those readers who would like more details about the Shroud of Turin should read *Verdict on the Shroud*, by Kenneth Stevenson and Gary Habermas (Wayne, Penn: Banbury Books, 1981) and an earlier book by Ian Wilson titled *The Shroud of Turin* (Garden City, N.Y.: Doubleday and Company, 1979).
2. Stevenson and Habermas, *Verdict*, p. 206.

and when there was indication of a miraculous removal of the body, the forces began to line up on the other side. That was nothing new.

In 1902, Yves Delage, an agnostic professor of comparative anatomy at the Sorbonne, became convinced that the corpse in the shroud was none other than the historic Jesus. When Delage made his findings known to the French Academy of Sciences, many of his colleagues were outraged that he would even discuss the subject, and the Academy refused to publish his work. Delage was understandably surprised and hurt. More recently, numerous articles and editorials, including one in the *New York Times*, have been critical of the authenticity of the shroud and the validity of the Shroud of Turin Research Project.

One magazine, *National Review*, did a generally favorable article on the shroud, and the response they received from their readers was immediate and harsh. In his "Notes and Asides" column, William F. Buckley answered:

> As for us, we fail to understand the manifest hostility toward the Shroud on the part of some Christians. Would they be equally interested or ostensibly uninterested in a possible or problem portrait of Xerxes? of Alexander the Great? Is it possible that the details of the Shroud are just too "literal" for an enlightened liberal sensibility? Is it somehow bad manners to suggest that Christian claims about what happened to Jesus are, in fact, true?[3]

The Nature of Unbelief

You need to understand that I wrote none of the above to suggest that faith in the resurrection of Christ is dependent on the authenticity of the Shroud of Turin. Instead, I wanted to underline the fact that most people don't believe in the resurrection, and if they were confronted with absolute, factual verification of the event, they still would not believe in it. To be sure, most people don't have trouble believing a "spiritual" resurrection or believing the resurrection is a myth that teaches

3. Stevenson and Habermas, *Verdict*, p. 233.

truth, but to believe that a dead man actually got out of the grave is another thing altogether. C. S. Lewis once said he knew only one person who claimed to have seen a ghost, and she didn't believe in immortality.

Here is the point: if the resurrection of Christ is not an absolute, space-time fact, then the whole Christian faith is silly. Paul put it this way, "If Christ has not been raised, your faith is worthless; you are still in your sins" (1 Cor. 15:17). Make no mistake about it, the resurrection of Christ is important, because the whole superstructure of the Christian faith is built on the assertion that Jesus didn't stay dead. And if He didn't, the implications are fantastic. If He did, on the other hand, you need to get as much of what this world offers as you possibly can in the time you have left. There is nothing else.

Unbelief That Denies Facts

Unbelief fascinates me, especially unbelief that denies facts to the detriment of the unbeliever. You would think the news that a man rose from the dead and said we could, too, would be seen as good news. You would think the news of the resurrection would be greeted with laughter and joy. But, as incredible as it seems, some people stand on the sidelines and throw rocks and shout, "I don't believe it, I won't believe it, and there is nothing you can say to me that will cause me to believe it."

It is the kind of unbelief found in the Bible. A case in point is the reaction of the religious establishment in dealing with the ressurrection of Christ. In Matthew 27:62–65, there is a curious reaction to even the possibility of the resurrection:

Now on the next day, which is the one after the preparation, the chief priests and the Pharisees gathered together with Pilate, and said, "Sir, we remember that when He [Jesus] was still alive that deceiver said, 'After three days I am to rise again.' Therefore, give orders for the grave to be made secure until the third day, lest the disciples come and steal Him away and say to the people, 'He has risen from the dead,' and the last deception will be worse than the first." Pilate said to them, "You have a guard; go, make it as secure as you know how." And they went and made the grave secure, and along with the guard they set a seal on the stone.

After the resurrection, Matthew recorded,

> Now while they were on their way, behold, some of the guard came into the city and reported to the chief priests all that had happened. [An angel had come to the tomb and struck the soldiers unconscious, and when they had regained consciousness Jesus was gone.] And when they had assembled with the elders and counseled together, they gave a large sum of money to the soldiers, and said, "You are to say, 'His disciples came by night and stole Him away while we were asleep.' " (Matt. 28:11-13)

A part of the ministry God has given me is a ministry to skeptics. I was one for so long that I determined that if I ever found some honest answers to my honest questions, I was going to share them with others who had honest questions. But the problem with the chief priests was that they didn't have any questions. They had the answers, and nothing was going to change their minds. I don't know the reason; perhaps it was a vested interest; maybe it was a fear of being wrong. But whatever the reason, the kind of unbelief the priests manifested was *unexamined* unbelief. After dealing with skeptics for a number of years and after being one for just as many years, I have found that a closed, skeptical mind is one of the great wonders of the world.

Somehow we have accepted the idea that fanaticism is the particular malady of the religious. That simply isn't true. You haven't seen anything until you have met a close-minded skeptic. At least a close-minded Christian has some hope and meaning. A close-minded skeptic has to fight to remain miserable. The chief priests sealed the tomb without the possibility (much less the hope) that a dead man was going to get out of the tomb on His own power. Not only that, but when they heard the truth of what had happened from those who were there, they still refused to believe. If they had examined the soldiers' story, they would have been confronted with a surprise of monumental proportions. But, you see, close-minded people never check.

Unbelief That Is Uncertain

There is another kind of unbelief, however, that is dear to the heart of God. That sort of unbelief was in a man named Thomas. You will remember that he was one of the disciples who had given his life to following Christ. After Jesus had been placed in the tomb, Thomas, like the others, was broken. Everything had come apart, and the devastation in his life was beyond calculation. Then, one evening, Jesus appeared to the disciples. Mind you, He was no ghost. He was the real Jesus who would eat a meal and teach a lesson. As you can imagine, it was an exciting revelation, but Thomas wasn't with the disciples at the time.

John recounted the incident: "The other disciples therefore were saying to him, 'We have seen the Lord!' But he said to them, 'Unless I shall see in His hands the imprint of the nails, and put my finger into the place of the nails, and put my hand into His side, I will not believe' " (John 20:25).

Thomas boiled in the juices of his own doubt for eight days. I can imagine that those eight days were horrible. The questions must have haunted him: *what if Jesus did come back from the dead? Can I afford to invest in any more hope? Where will I go to find some answers?* I suspect that each time Thomas got to the point of hope, he closed his eyes and heard the hammer driving the nails through Jesus' hands and thought to himself, *I just can't go through the loss again.*

The next time Jesus appeared to the disciples, however, Thomas was with them:

> Jesus came, the doors having been shut, and stood in their midst, and said, "Peace be with you." Then He said to Thomas, "Reach here your finger, and see My hands; and reach here your hand, and put it into My side; and be not unbelieving, but believing." Thomas answered and said to Him, "My Lord and my God!" Jesus said to him, "Because you have seen Me, have you believed? Blessed are they who did not see, and yet believed." (John 20:26b–29)

We sometimes have "Skeptics Forum" at our church. It is a group of unbelievers who meet to see if the Christian faith is true. I am the only Christian among them, and the skeptics set the agenda. The sessions go for about ten weeks, and each session deals with one question, such as, does God exist? Is the Bible true? How do you explain suffering if you have a compassionate God? I usually speak to the question for about ten minutes, and then for the next two hours the skeptics go after me. I could fill the rest of this book with incidents that have happened in "Skeptics Forum," but one of the most moving incidents happened the evening a young woman began to cry. She was a teacher who had given up the Christian faith as a teenager. I asked her the reason for her tears, and she said, "Oh God, I wish this stuff were true." Thomas was like that, and God met his questions with answers that absolutely took his breath away.

Unbelief That Is Unaware

There is another kind of unbelief we ought to consider before leaving the subject. It is the unbelief that is unaware. In Luke 24, you will remember, there were two travelers on the road to a village called Emmaus, which was seven miles from Jerusalem. The crucifixion of Jesus had taken place three days before, and they were discussing the rumor of Jesus' resurrection. Let me allow Luke to tell the story:

> And it came about that while they were conversing and discussing, Jesus Himself approached, and began traveling with them. But their eyes were prevented from recognizing Him. And He said to them, "What are these words that you are exchanging with one another as you are walking?" And they stood still, looking sad. And one of them, named Cleopas, answered and said to Him, "Are you the only one visiting Jerusalem and unaware of the things which have happened here in these days?" (Luke 24:15–18)

The two men then explained to Jesus all that had happened, including the reports from those who had seen Jesus after He had risen from the dead. Luke continued:

And He [Jesus] said to them, "O foolish men and slow of heart to believe in all that the prophets have spoken! Was it not necessary for the Christ to suffer these things and to enter into His glory?" And beginning with Moses and with all the prophets, He explained to them the things concerning Himself in all the Scriptures. And they approached the village where they were going, and He acted as though He would go farther. And they urged Him, saying, "Stay with us, for it is getting toward evening, and the day is now nearly over." And He went in to stay with them. And it came about that when He had reclined at table with them, He took the bread and blessed it, and breaking it, He began giving it to them. And their eyes were opened and they recognized Him; and He vanished from their sight. And they said to one another, "Were not our hearts burning within us while He was speaking to us on the road, while He was explaining the Scriptures to us?" And they arose that very hour and returned to Jerusalem, and found gathered together the eleven and those who were with them, saying, "The Lord has really risen, and has appeared to Simon." And they began to relate their experiences on the road and how He was recognized by them in the breaking of the bread. (Luke 24:25–35)

My friend Tom Haggai, who was a friend of the famous Baptist pastor Robert G. Lee, told me one time why Lee was such a great evangelist. Early in his ministry, Dr. Lee was awakened one evening by a phone call telling him about a young woman in her twenties who had taken an overdose of drugs. The caller told Dr. Lee she was in the hospital and was dying. He asked Dr. Lee if he would come.

Dr. Lee went to visit the woman. He came close to her bed, bent over her dying body, and said, "My dear, I'm Pastor Lee, and I have come to talk to you."

"Oh Dr. Lee," she said, "I have heard you preach many times."

"I'm glad," he replied, "but I have come to talk to you about Christ. I would like you to receive Christ as your Savior."

"Dr. Lee," she said, "I have heard you preach many times."

"My dear," he persisted, "you are close to death, and it is of eternal importance that you receive Christ."

"Dr. Lee," she again said, "I have heard you preach many

times." He determined that if anyone heard him preach again, they would remember what they needed to know about Christ.

The dying woman and the two travelers on the road to Emmaus are examples of unbelief based on a lack of knowledge. It is unbelief that is unaware.

And thus, in regard to the resurrection of Christ, we have three kinds of unbelief; unbelief that is unexamined, unbelief that is uncertain, and unbelief that is unaware. The first kind of unbelief must simply be ignored. For some reason, we Christians seem to think we ought to give ourselves to those who would rather be left alone. But if time is limited (and it is), if there are those who have already made up their minds despite the facts (and there are), and if there are people who really want to know the truth (and there are), then we ought to waste as little time as possible on those whose unbelief is unexamined.

However, it is terribly important that all unbelievers hear the truth. Let me give you some facts if you are an unbeliever.

Facts about the Resurrection

Fact No. 1: The disciples of Jesus of Nazareth were changed because something happened that absolutely "blew their minds." They claimed they had seen Jesus—after He died. It is possible, I suppose, to deny that they saw Jesus after His death, but it is impossible to say they didn't see something. Too much changed to deny that.

If you will, go with me to the upper room where the disciples gathered after the death of Christ. There never was a more depressed group of men. Everything for which they had worked and prayed had come to an abrupt end on the town garbage heap between two thieves. The dreams of a lifetime were in dust at their feet. Jesus was dead. Peter said, "I'm going fishing." That's all there was left to do. Matthew would return to his tax tables, James and John to their fishing business, and Nathanael to his dreaming. They would remember the days when He lived; they would remember and be sad for what might have been. They would go back to their old lives as sadder but wiser men.

They were afraid, too. When you watch a man die in agony on a cross, the thing you say to yourself is that you never want it to happen to you. There are no good ways to die, but if you had a choice, crucifixion would not be it. Suppose you had been a follower of Jesus and you had watched Him die. It would dawn on you that the leaders didn't like you a whole lot more than they liked Him. Then you would think, *It could happen to me, too.* And so these disciples gathered in the upper room because when you are afraid it is better to be afraid with someone else.

But think of these men only a few days later on the day of Pentecost. Were these the same men who huddled together in that upper room? They looked the same; they had the same accents, the same names—but they weren't the same. Peter, for instance, the coward who had denied Christ three times, stood before a crowd of thousands and spoke in a booming, assured voice:

> Men of Judea, and all you who live in Jerusalem, let this be known to you, and give heed to my words.... Men of Israel, listen to these words: Jesus the Nazarene, a Man attested to you by God with miracles and wonders and signs which God performed through Him in your midst, just as you yourselves know—this Man, delivered up by the predetermined plan and foreknowledge of God, you nailed to a cross by the hands of godless men and put Him to death. And God raised Him up again, putting an end to the agony of death, since it was impossible for Him to be held in its power. (Acts 2:14b, 22–24)

That, I would submit, was not the same Peter who wouldn't take a stand before the crucifixion.

The question then is this: what caused the change? And consider what they *didn't* say after they had changed: "We have some nice things to say about a martyr who was a great teacher." No, they didn't proclaim a new, wonderful teaching about love. They didn't talk about religion. They said they had seen a dead man walking! They said they had eaten with Him, talked to Him, and touched Him. That is a fact that requires explanation.

Fact No. 2: The disciples were willing to die for their claim that they had seen Jesus after His death. Of the original disciples, only John died of old age, and he was exiled to the island of Patmos. Tradition says James was run through with the sword, and Peter was crucified upside-down because he said he was not worthy to die as his Master had died.

Now let me ask you a question: would you insist on a lie if you knew it took you one step closer to death every time you told it? Would you really participate in a conspiracy designed to bring about your own death, and a horrible death at that? Would you really nail a nail into your own coffin if you knew you could prevent it? Of course you wouldn't! Jesus' disciples wouldn't have, either, but they were willing to die for their claim. That is a fact that needs an explanation.

Fact No. 3: The disciples were not the only ones who saw Jesus after His death. There were more than five hundred people who saw Him. If one person told us he had seen a man getting out of a grave, we would call the medics in white jackets. If two people told us a dead man had gotten up and walked, we would reply, "You've got to be kidding!" If ten people told us they had just come from a graveyard where a dead man had risen from a grave, we probably wouldn't believe them, but at least we would go down to the graveyard and check. But if five hundred people told us the same story, we would have to give serious consideration to their testimonies.

I once was the pastor in a little village on Cape Cod. One of the members of the church was the parks commissioner for the village. There wasn't much for a parks commissioner to do except mow the graveyard and keep the hedges trimmed. On one occasion, this man was cleaning off a headstone over a grave that was more than a hundred years old. A hundred years ago, no one required "grave liners"; so the old graves had a tendency to cave in. On this occasion the grave gave way, and he fell into the hole. He told me later that as he was climbing out of the hole, someone drove through the cemetery and saw him.

Whoever was driving the car thought my friend was coming out of a grave and couldn't drive out of the graveyard fast enough. (My friend couldn't see who it was, he was driving so fast.)

What if that man had come to the church and told us what he had seen? We would have kidded him and then explained what had really happened. But if five hundred people (see 1 Cor. 15:6) see a dead man walking and they tell you not only that they saw Him alive after they had seen Him die, but also that they talked to Him—you wonder. That is a fact that needs some explanation.

Fact No. 4: The religious and governmental institutions had a vested interest in stopping the rapid spread of the Christian faith, but they could not do it. By the fourth century Christians had conquered the Roman Empire. The Christian faith had swept away the government that had tried to persecute it out of existence. Now, let me ask you a question: why didn't they stop the spread of Christianity? It should have been a relatively simple matter. The leaders could have gone down to the cemetery and brought the corpse forth for everyone to see, but they didn't. I'm going to tell you the reason they didn't: there was no corpse! The dead body had gotten up and walked away. The leaders who most wanted to destroy the Christian faith couldn't do it. That is a fact that needs an explanation.

Fact No. 5: The witnesses to the resurrection of Jesus in the first century were credible witnesses or their testimonies would not have held up. We live in a provincial age whose people believe that every age but ours was superstitious and credulous. We think we are the only generation that ever had doubts. That's silly, of course, and we ought to remember that first-century people had just as many doubts as we have about corpses getting out of graves. However, they had an advantage over us. They were able to talk to the witnesses. They could cross-examine them, check out their facts, and make sure their stories held water. If their testimonies hadn't held up, the Christian faith would have died in the first century. It didn't. That is a fact that needs an explanation.

Fact No. 6: The church of Christ covered the Western world by the fourth century. There were simply no rivals. Let me ask you another question: do you seriously believe that a religious movement built on a lie could accomplish that much? It is said that when Augustine was informed about the fall of Rome, he was saddened. But he said, "I am the citizen of a city that shall never fall." Out of the ruins of Rome, Augustine fashioned his monumental work *The City of God.* How do you explain the phenomenal growth of the Christian church? It is a fact that needs explanation.

Of course, these are only a few of the facts surrounding the resurrection of Jesus Christ. I would suggest the interested reader pursue the matter further. Frank Morrison's *Who Moved The Stone?* and Josh McDowell's *Evidence that Demands a Verdict,* Vol. 1, can be obtained at any Christian bookstore and are good popular works on the subject.

The Importance of the Resurrection

So what? If Jesus did get up out of the grave (and He did), what difference does it make? It makes a lot of difference! It means that everything He said is true, that the teaching He gave is practical, that the life He lived and lives can make your life different. Let's talk about the difference Christ's resurrection makes in terms of the fact that we're going to die and are afraid of death.

Death is an awesome reality, and it is one with which most of us would rather not deal. We do everything possible to cover it up, to hide its reality. Our culture, for instance, has become expert in the art of making a corpse look alive. How often have you heard someone standing at an open coffin say, "My, Sam [or Sally or Joe] really looks good." He doesn't look good! He's dead! We cover the corpse with polished wood, heap it with flowers, dim the lighting, and place it in a beautiful setting. We do everything possible to hide the reality that someone is a corpse.

How much better it was when the family had to do all the "dirty" work of preparing the loved one for burial. The family made the coffin, laid out the corpse, used their home for the wake, dug the hole, and buried the loved one. That may seem harsh, but psychologically it was very healthy. People faced the reality of death and were able to deal with it. Grief was hard work, but it was short. Today years sometimes pass before a family fully recovers from a loss.

Be that as it may, we don't want to think about death. And when we do, we usually say something silly like, "Death is a normal part of living" or "Just like birth, death is natural."

Let me tell you something important: death is not normal. You were not created to die. In fact, the Bible teaches that you were created to live forever. When Jesus died on the cross and rose from the dead, He did it so you could fulfill your eternal destiny of living forever.

Paul made a startling statement in his first letter to the Corinthians:

> Now I say this, brethren, that flesh and blood cannot inherit the kingdom of God; nor does the perishable inherit the imperishable. Behold, I tell you a mystery; we shall not all sleep [i.e., die], but we shall all be changed, in a moment, in the twinkling of an eye, at the last trumpet; for the trumpet will sound, and the dead will be raised imperishable, and we shall be changed. For this perishable must put on the imperishable, and this mortal must put on immortality. But when this perishable will have put on the imperishable, and this mortal will have put on immortality, then will come about the saying that is written, "Death is swallowed up in victory. O death, where is your victory? O death, where is your sting?" The sting of death is sin, and the power of sin is the law; but thanks be to God, who gives us the victory through our Lord Jesus Christ. Therefore, my beloved brethren, be steadfast, immovable, always abounding in the work of the Lord, knowing that your toil is not in vain in the Lord. (1 Cor. 15:50–58)

Do you know why you have to die? You have to die because you have sinned. The Bible says that the wages of sin is death (see Rom. 6:23). That isn't something anyone likes, but nevertheless, it's still true. If you jump off a fifteen-story building, you are going to kill yourself. If you put your hand on a hot stove, you are going to get burned. If you sin, you are going to die. On the cross, Jesus took our sin and declared us forgiven. The penalty of sin (death) has been borne by Christ for us. Because the sin is gone, the death is gone. And Jesus came back from the grave to prove it.

Jesus said, "After a little while the world will behold Me no more; but you will behold Me; because I live, you shall live also" (John 14:19). If Jesus stayed in the grave, the first part of His statement is not true; and therefore, it follows logically that the second part of His statement is not true either. If Jesus did not live, then we won't. But if He did live, if He got up out of the grave, if He broke the bonds of death, then *we will, too*. He promised, and He is the only one who has the right and the knowledge to make that promise.

The next time you face the fact of your death or the death of someone you loved who knew Jesus, don't hide its reality. Death is not a very pretty sight. The next time you have to face that reality, don't cover it up—fight it with the truth. Death has died, and death died at the hands of the Prince who has given immortality to those who follow Him. That is a fact, and you can hang your hat on it.

9 A HERITAGE OF FORGIVENESS

If Jesus has come...
I am clean.

In Him we have redemption through His blood, the forgiveness of our trespasses, according to the riches of His grace which He lavished upon us.
Ephesians 1:7-8a

A few years ago I was speaking at a conference, and I told about how I had been a pastor before I knew God. After the session, a man came up to me with an obvious question. "Steve," he asked, "if you didn't know God, why, in God's name, did you go into the ministry?" I didn't have an answer for him that evening, but I've thought about the question a lot since then.

There are several reasons why someone who doesn't know God goes into the ministry. For instance, someone can enter the ministry because he or she would like to know God. Religious friends told me I had a glib tongue and would be a good preacher. I was interested in philosophy, and there wasn't much of a market for philosophers. I had a vague desire to help people, and every preference test I ever took showed I was high in the particular proclivities that would make a good pastor. But, to be perfectly honest with you, the main reason I entered the ministry was to allay guilt.

A lot of the guilt I felt I didn't have to feel. It was a psychological, undefined, unproductive guilt. Nevertheless, it hurt just as much as the real thing. Real guilt is based on a real violation of God's standard, and real guilt needs real repentance. When the repentance takes place there is a sense of relief and freedom. "For the sorrow that is according to the will of God produces a repentance without regret, leading to salvation; but the sorrow of the world produces death" (2 Cor. 7:10). I had real, definable guilt, too, and I felt necessarily guilty about a lot of things.

My guilt caused me to turn to a profession where I could be a "good" person and perhaps feel better about myself. Now, I am sure that I have been called to be a pastor. I'm doing what God told me to do, and if He used guilt to motivate me to do His will, I'm glad. He didn't check with me first. But motivation by guilt presents some serious problems, not the least of which is the fact that guilty people make others feel guilty. And in case you haven't noticed, the best way to get people to do church work is to make them feel guilty. It's always easy to get people involved in evangelism, visiting, stewardship, or anything else by making them feel guilty. Of course, their motivation doesn't last very long, but it certainly gets them started. As I read back over the sermons I preached in those early days, I blush to see that I had become a master of motivating people with guilt.

Then I noticed an amazing change in the content of my sermons. Somewhere in the early years of my ministry, I stopped trying to make people feel guilty. I know the reason I changed: I discovered that God is a great forgiver. I learned what it really means to be forgiven. I understood what Christ did for me on the cross. I didn't feel guilty anymore; therefore, I didn't have to make others feel guilty anymore. I didn't have to manipulate people anymore. I didn't have to assuage my guilt by getting others to share it. I was free.

Please understand me. There is legitimate guilt. A lot of folks who don't feel guilty ought to. When Christians (or unbelievers, for that matter) violate God's law, they ought to feel guilty. I'm not saying that we don't have to talk about sin anymore. What I'm saying is that if truth is taught, the Holy Spirit will do the convicting (see John 16:8), not us. When the Holy Spirit convicts people, He always does it for the right reasons.

In Matthew 5:17–18 Jesus said, "Do not think that I came to abolish the Law or the Prophets; I did not come to abolish, but to fulfill. For truly I say to you, until heaven and earth pass away, not the smallest letter or stroke shall pass away from the Law, until all is accomplished."

Did Jesus change the law? Of course not. If you want to know what God wants you to do, all you have to do is check the law. When the Jews say that the law, the Holy Torah, is the greatest gift God ever gave, they are right. It is a tremendous thing to know what God wants from His creatures. If, for instance, I don't know what my boss wants me to do in my job, I'm going to have some serious problems. I will always have an overwhelming sense of anxiety about whether or not I am doing the job I have been hired to do. So, accurate information about how I am to do my job is important. And if that's true about my job, it's much more true about how I'm to live my life.

God reflects His information not only on the right way to live, but also on the best way to live. The law tells us where life's minefields are. It tells us the best way to live in order to have reasonably balanced and happy lives.

This raises an obvious question: if all that is true about the law of God, and if Jesus didn't come to change the law, what did He do about the law? Listen! He came to give us two important gifts, power and forgiveness—power to obey the law, and forgiveness when we don't. Wouldn't it be nice to have the power to be different from what you are right now? Wouldn't you like to have power over sin? These questions are an advertisement for the next chapter, where we will talk about the amazing example that Prince Jesus has given to His own.

Necessary Bad News

For the rest of this chapter I want to talk to you about the second of those gifts, forgiveness. But you can't talk about forgiveness unless you talk about why there is a need for forgiveness. That means you can't hear the good news until you hear the bad news. The bad news is that, believe it or not, you are not a good person. Remember the verse we read from Jeremiah?

"The heart is more deceitful than all else and is desperately sick; who can understand it?" (Jer. 17:9). The Bible also says, "We have already charged that both Jews and Greeks are all under sin; as it is written, 'There is none righteous, not even one; there is none who understands, there is none who seeks for God; all have turned aside, together they have become useless; there is none who does good, there is not even one' " (Rom. 3:9b–12). "If we say that we have no sin, we are deceiving ourselves, and the truth is not in us" (1 John 1:8). What the Bible says about us isn't very nice; nevertheless, it is true.

My friend Fred Smith says that there are two basic anthropological views, two views of man that determine everything we think and do in education, government, and the church. The first view is that man is basically good with a proclivity for evil, and the second is that man is basically bad with a proclivity for good. If you believe the first of the two propositions, you may believe in democracy, for instance, because people are good and can be trusted. If you believe in the second proposition, you may believe in democracy because people aren't good and no one person is good enough to have too much power.

In *The Federalist*, Alexander Hamilton defended the idea of a union as opposed to separate nations living in close harmony with one another:

> A man must be far gone in Utopian speculations who can seriously doubt that, if these States should either be wholly disunited, or only united impartial confederacies, the subdivisions into which they might be thrown would have frequent and violent contests with each other. To presume a want of motives for such contests as an argument against their existence, would be to forget that men are ambitious, vindictive, and rapacious. To look for a continuation of harmony between a number of independent, unconnected sovereignties in the same neighbourhood, would be to disregard the uniform course of human events, and to set at defiance the accumulated experience of ages.[1]

---

1. Alexander Hamilton, James Madison, John Jay, *The Federalist*, Great Books of the Western World, Robert Hutchins, ed. (Chicago: Encyclopaedia Britannica, 1952), p. 39.

One of the interesting things about liberal Christianity is that it believes idealistically in the perfectability of human nature. The reason liberal Christianity is dying is that an institution built on a lie eventually dies. When all the restraints of society, religion, and culture are removed, human nature is not very pretty. I love C. S. Lewis's designation of earth as "the silent planet" in his science fiction. If you haven't read the *Space Trilogy*, you should. Lewis suggested that all the other planets of the universe are without redemption because they didn't need to be redeemed. One planet, the earth, is fallen and dark. It is the silent planet.

That is an accurate description of earth. In all of human history, earth has enjoyed only a few years of relative peace. It has been a planet rife with selfishness, strife, ambition, and war; a planet where *holocaust* is not a word for one historical incident but for many: Cambodia, Turkey, Germany, to name a few. There is something warped about our planet and its people, something bent, and any philosophical, political, social, or religious system that fails to take that into account is doomed to failure.

Author William Golding clearly shows us the degeneracy of human nature. In *Lord of the Flies*, a group of boys is stranded on a deserted island and civilized behavior deteriorates into chaos, destruction, and murder. It is an accurate assessment of the way things really are.

Let's get a little more personal. There was a time in my life when I believed there were two kinds of people in the world: good people and bad people. The good people went to church on Sunday, were honest in their dealings with others, didn't cheat on their wives or husbands, and didn't smoke or drink too much. The bad people were those who had turned away from God, were dishonest in their dealings with others, cheated on their wives or husbands, and smoked and drank too much. I wasn't a pastor long before I discovered I was right that there are two kinds of people in the world, but I was wrong about who they are. Actually, there are bad people who know they're bad, and there are bad people who don't. You fall into one or the other of those categories.

The Big Ten

I suspect the best way to determine whether we're sinners is to review the "Big Ten," the Ten Commandments. People are always saying to me that they have made a few mistakes but that they certainly are not *bad*. I have found it helpful to get out my Bible, turn to Exodus 20, and go over the requirements of God.

The first commandment God gave the world was not to have any other gods before Him (see Exod. 20:3). "Well," you say, "I certainly haven't violated that commandment. I have been brought up in the church worshiping the true God; I had godly parents who taught me the truth about the true God; I never have been involved in any religious movement where any other god was worshiped." But wait, and think for a moment. Have you ever placed your job, your family, or your desires above God?

The Westminster Larger Catechism says this about the first commandment:

> The duties required in the first commandment are: the knowing and acknowledging of God to be the only true God, and our God [okay so far]; and to worship and glorify Him accordingly [still okay]; by thinking, meditating, remembering, highly esteeming, honoring, adoring, choosing, loving, desiring, fearing of Him; believing Him; trusting, hoping, delighting, rejoicing in Him; [how are you doing?] being zealous for Him; calling upon Him, giving all praise and thanks, and yielding all obedience and submission to Him with the whole man; being careful in all things to please Him, and sorrowful when in anything He is offended; and walking humbly with Him.

You say you have some trouble with all of that? Guilty!

In His second commandment, God told us we should not make any graven images and worship them. "Well," you say, "I don't even know what a graven image is, and if I did I'm sure I wouldn't bother with one." But have you ever bought a new house or a new car and been so pleased with it that you placed it above God? Have you ever bowed down in your heart before a movie star or a rock idol? Have you ever created a god in your heart that was not the God of the Bible, perhaps a god who makes no demands but promises to bless you, and felt good about your creation? Have you ever thought that maybe, just maybe, there was power in a cross you hung around your neck or a rabbit foot you carried in your pocket? Guilty!

The third commandment said we should never take the name of God in vain. "Well," you say, "I certainly don't swear." Maybe not, but have you ever promised God something you didn't deliver? Have you ever prayed a prayer or sung a hymn that you didn't mean? Have you ever portrayed yourself as a godly person without living as one? Guilty!

The fourth commandment said we are to keep and honor the Sabbath day. "Well," you say, "maybe I haven't always done that." As a matter of fact, it could be that you have violated this commandment more than you think. Do you set aside one day, twenty-four hours, a week for God? How about setting aside eight hours a week, or two, or one? Have you ever violated the body God gave you as a gift, by refusing to give your body rest? Have you ever decided that playing golf, going fishing, or sleeping was more important than the worship of God in the presence of His people? (Someone tells the story about the pastor who wanted to play golf on a Sunday morning. He got his associate to preach for him, while he went out on the links. He had the best game of his life. In fact, he got three holes in one. God said to an angel who was rather upset that the pastor would play golf on Sunday during the worship hour, "See, I have exacted the proper punishment. Three holes in one, and he won't be able to tell a single soul.") Have you ever made the Sabbath profane by profaning God's day with your profane actions? Guilty!

The fifth commandment said we are to honor our fathers and mothers. Think about the way you have treated your parents. Think about the times you were disobedient, made fun of their "old-fashioned" ways, or talked about them behind their backs. Have you turned away from the values taught by your mother or father? Have you ever been ashamed of them? Have you ever felt you carry the emotional baggage placed on you by your parents? Guilty!

The sixth commandment said we should not kill (literally,

murder). "Well," you say, "I'm certainly no murderer." Perhaps
you have never killed anyone with a knife or a gun, but have
you ever killed someone with your words? Have you ever been
the causative factor in someone's turning away from God?
Have you ever ignored a brother or a sister, laughed at his efforts and criticized his ways? Have you ever been the person
who created the loneliness in another's heart or promoted sin in
another's life? Have you ever failed to give witness of the gospel
of Christ? Have you ever remained silent in the face of hunger,
racism, or oppression? Have you ever looked at a hungry,
frightened, desperate world and turned away? Guilty!

The seventh commandment instructed us not to commit
adultery. Jesus said in Matthew 5:27-28 that the seventh commandment prohibits more than sexual intercourse; lust is adulterous, too. Have you ever desired a sexual relationship with
someone other than your husband or wife? Have you ever wondered what it would be like to cheat a little bit? Have you ever
fantasized about an adulterous relationship or dreamed about
one? In his *Confessions*, Augustine was frustrated by his memory
of sexual sin. He cried out, "Great is the power of memory, a
fearful thing, O my God, a deep and boundless manifoldness;
and this thing is the mind, and this am I myself. What am I
then, O my God?"[2] And in his essay "On Marriage and Concupiscence," Augustine said, "For the concupiscence of the
flesh is in some sort active, even when it does not exhibit as as-
sent of the heart, where its seat of empire is, or those members
whereby, as its weapons, it fulfills what it is bent on."[3] Have you
ever allowed your mind to wander through forbidden fields of
sexual fantasy? Guilty!

The eighth commandment teaches us not to steal. "At least,"
you say, "I'm no thief." No? Have you always been faithful to
God's requirements of stewardship? Have you always given
your financial assistance when you could afford it? Have you
ever used God's money for something else? A millionaire was

2. Augustine, *The Confessions*, Great Books of the Western World, Robert
Hutchins, ed. (Chicago: Encyclopaedia Britannica, 1952), p. 78.
3. *The Nicene and Post-Nicene Fathers*, vol. 5, *St. Augustine* (Grand Rapids: Wm. B.
Eerdmans Publishing Company, 1971), p. 276.

giving a testimony to a congregation about the importance of stewardship, and to inspire the troops, he told of an incident that happened when he was a boy. He said there was a missionary at his church who was in desperate need of money. On that occasion he had only fifty cents. It was all that he had in the world, but, he said, "Moved by God's Spirit, when the offering plate came by I put in that fifty cents. Ladies and gentlemen, I gave everything I had." The man went back to his pew and sat down, whereupon an elderly woman sitting behind him leaned over and said in a stage whisper, "I dare you to do it again." Have you ever sacrificed for God's work? Have you ever robbed God of the time you ought to be giving Him, or of your talents? Guilty!

The ninth commandment said we should never bear false witness against anyone. "I wouldn't do that," you say. Maybe. Have you always been truthful about what you have said about others? Have you ever told only half the truth? Have you ever kept quiet when your brother or sister needed defending? Have you ever allowed an untruth to be told about another? Have you ever given someone the impression that you knew something you didn't know about another person? Guilty!

And then the final commandment of the Big Ten: God said we should not covet. In other words, envy is wrong in the eyes of God. Only the very foolish or the very dishonest would not admit to the sin of envy. It's around us every day; it stares at us from our neighbors' garages; it glitters in the department store windows; it leaps up and laughs at us in the considerable gifts of our brothers' ministries. Envy haunts us at night when we try to sleep, and it tells us that life's not fair. The preachers call it ecclesiastical and denominational differences, and the business community calls it competitive motivation—but it's still envy.

There was once a rooster who went into the ostrich pen and got one of the gigantic eggs. He rolled it over to his pen, pushed it in front of the hens, and said, "Now, I don't want you to think I'm complaining, but I did want you to see what the competition is doing." Envy runs throughout the fabric of our lives. Guilty!

Of course we could spend considerable time talking about

what God requires from us for the poor and oppressed; we could talk about how hard Jesus was on the sins of anger and pride; we could quote Paul on forgiveness, faithfulness, and love; we could speak of witnessing and evangelism, or integrity and honor. But if none of that makes the point, then maybe Jesus' words will make us see: "Therefore you are to be perfect, as your heavenly Father is perfect" (Matt. 5:48).

The bad news is this: you and I are sinners. We have enough selfishness and pride in our hearts to destroy the good that is there. All the superficial and shallow talk about "self-image" and "moral perfectability" will not change the fact that there is something seriously wrong at the very heart of things. There is something bent about human nature. James was not one to mince words. He said,

> What is the source of quarrels and conflicts among you? Is not the source your pleasures that wage war in your members? You lust and do not have; so you commit murder. And you are envious and cannot obtain; so you fight and quarrel. You do not have because you do not ask. You ask and do not receive, because you ask with wrong motives, so that you may spend it on your pleasures. (James 4:1–3)

Sin's Effect

"All right," you say, "so I'm not such a good person. Big deal! I'm only human." I wish that were the only truth. Unfortunately, there is more to the bad news than what I've told you so far. Sin isn't just something you do that is human and makes no difference. Sin does things to you that conflict with the way you were created to be.

God doesn't sit in heaven and say, "Everytime one of My creatures finds something interesting, fun, and exciting to do, I'm going to call it a sin, because I want to make My creatures miserable." Instead, God wants us to be obedient, so that we might live as fulfilled lives as possible. Benjamin Franklin was not known for his Christian commitment, but he spoke a biblical truth when he said, "Sin is not hurtful because it is forbidden, but it is forbidden because it is hurtful. Nor is duty beneficial because it is commanded, but it is commanded because it is beneficial."

It is important that we see what sin does to us. Have you ever blushed privately thinking about something you had done? Have you ever been robbed of sleep because your guilt was eating you alive? I heard recently about a young woman who said she knew she had become a Christian because of the bed sheets. When asked how that let her know about her salvation, she replied that before she was a Christian they were always twisted and disheveled, but after she came to know Christ she would wake up in the morning with the sheets smooth and straight. She smiled and said, "I sleep better."

I think it was in one of A. J. Cronin's stories that a certain doctor worked for one company for most of his career. He started out with high aspirations and a genuine desire to help people. But as the years went by, he sold his soul little by little. He started drinking and became a self-centered, bitter man. His wife died, and after her death he was going through her pocketbook. He found letters from people he had helped and some pictures of himself when he was a young, idealistic doctor. He walked to a mirror, looked at the man he had become, and said, "You thought you would get away with it, but, by God, you didn't."

Sin does more than just hurt us; it also divides us from other people. In your whole lifetime, you will be lucky if you have three or four good friends. We have lots of acquaintances but few friends, and do you know why? It's because we don't want that many people to know what we are really like. You see, we wear masks that hide the ugliness underneath. We show others our masks so they won't see the way we really are. There are only a few people who can see what is behind our masks and love us anyway. So our sin separates us from other people.

By far the most horrible consequence of sin is that it separates us from our holy God. I used to have a dance band in high school and college, and every time we played an engagement, we closed with the song, "He." I don't know if you remember that song, but it said a lot of insipid and sweet things about God, and its last line was that God always says, "I forgive."

That sounds good, but it just isn't true. God is not the kind of God portrayed by the shallow folk-religion of our day. He is the God of the universe who is holy and righteous. When He gives His commandments, He doesn't put them in the form of suggestions. When He says "The wages of sin is death," He means that those who sin will be separated from Him eternally. Paul said, "To those who are selfishly ambitious and do not obey the truth, but obey unrighteousness, wrath and indignation [will be the result]. There will be tribulation and distress for every soul of man who does evil, of the Jew first and also of the Greek" (Rom. 2:8–9).

It is very foolish to stand before the God of the universe and be flippant about sin. Isaiah knew better. You will remember that he was in the temple when he had a vision of God. He saw the Lord on a high throne, with His train filling the temple. In his vision, Isaiah saw heavenly beings surrounding God's throne, and the beings were calling back and forth to one another, "Holy, Holy, Holy, is the Lord of hosts, the whole earth is full of His glory" (Isa. 6:3). Isaiah didn't say, "Wow! Isn't that something!" He didn't say, "What a loving God!" He didn't say, "It is nice to have a personal encounter in my heart with a wonderful God." This is what he said: "Woe is me, for I am ruined! because I am a man of unclean lips, and I live among a people of unclean lips; for my eyes have seen the King, the Lord of hosts" (Isa. 6:5).

One of the reasons most people are miserable is that they were created to be in fellowship with their Creator yet they live outside Him. Augustine said, "Thou hast created us for Thyself, and our hearts are restless until they find their rest in Thee." Pascal said that we have a God-shaped vacuum in our hearts, and nothing fits in the vacuum except God. The problem is that our sin separates us from Him. He is infinite and we are finite; He is in heaven and we are on earth; He is holy and we are sinful. Our approach to the source of our joy, power, and forgiveness in God is blocked by sin. Don't let anybody tell you different. Paul cried out, "Wretched man that I am! Who will set me free from the body of this death?" (Rom. 7:24).

The Bible says that at the fall of Adam in the garden, a terrible disease entered into the world (see Rom. 5:12). It is a disease far more destructive than cancer, and it is universal. We sin because it has diseased us; it is in our blood. We sin because Adam sinned, but we also sin *as* Adam sinned. Almost all sin is first degree since we contemplated it and played with it long before we consumed it and made it a part of our lives. However, to know why we do something or to know why something hurts us doesn't necessarily help us with the problem. We return to sin again and again.

The Good News

Now let's talk about the good news. The Bible says, "For while we were still helpless, at the right time Christ died for the ungodly [that's everybody]. For one will hardly die for a righteous man; though perhaps for the good man someone would dare even to die. But God demonstrates His own love toward us, in that while we were yet sinners, Christ died for us" (Rom. 5:6–8).

Most of us have a superficial view of forgiveness. Forgiveness is a simple thing, right? Wrong. Forgiveness is very difficult, because whenever anyone is forgiven, someone gets hurt. Think about it for a moment. If I punch you in the nose, you can choose to forgive me or not. If you choose not to forgive me, you can punch me back and things will be balanced out. But if you decide to forgive me, it's going to cost you a punch in the nose. There is no such thing as cheap forgiveness—on our part or on God's part. Forgiveness always costs.

Our being forgiven cost God His Son. Jesus bore the cost of our sin on the cross. Paul said, "Therefore having been justified by faith, we have peace with God through our Lord Jesus Christ" (Rom. 5:1). That means you don't have to be guilty anymore. The relationship between you and God can be restored. You don't have to worry about bad self-image or death or hell. You can be totally, wonderfully, joyfully accepted and forgiven. Gert Behanna said that when she got up from her knees after confessing her sin before God and asking forgiveness because of Christ, she not only felt forgiven, but she also felt *welcomed*.

The bad news is that we are sinners. The good news is this: if the Prince has come, forgiveness has reality and we are clean. At the close of his life, John Newton said he could remember two things: "I am a great sinner and Jesus is a great Saviour." That's true, and it is exciting. I'm not okay, and you're not okay—but it's okay.

Why We Don't Feel Forgiven

And then we have one final question with which we must deal before we bring this subject to an end. If we are forgiven, why do we still feel guilty? There are so many Christians who have been forgiven who don't "feel" forgiven that it would be wrong to pass them by. Day after day I listen to confessions by Christians who ought not to be confessing. They have been carrying a burden of guilt for years, and they have been doing it needlessly. If you are in that position, the rest of this chapter is for you. If you still feel guilty when you ought not to feel guilty, I want to suggest the three "R's" of release from false guilt.

First, let me suggest that you readjust your thinking. The problem with many of us is that we have not truly understood forgiveness from God's standpoint. When you became a Christian, you were reconciled to God through the blood of Christ. The problem with many of us is that we see the reconciliation only in terms of forgiveness for past sins. But when you became a Christian you were made a child of God forever, not just until you did something bad.

Most of us think (and many of us pastors have fostered the image) of what Christ did for us in terms of a slate. When we became Christians, God wiped the slate of our past sins clean. Right? Wrong! When we became Christians, God didn't just wipe the slate clean. *He threw it away.*

You see, it is not the sin that is important anymore; it is the relationship, and the relationship is established forever. When my children were born, I knew from the beginning that they were going to be disobedient to me on occasions. I knew there would be times when I would see them doing wrong things. I knew from the time they were born that I could not expect perfection. And so I gave them up for adoption. Of course I didn't! They are my children, and there is nothing they can ever do to me or against me that will stop them from being my beloved children.

John 1:12 tells us that when we came to know Christ, we became children of the Father. That's settled, and we no longer need to try to earn God's favor. Confession never takes place for salvation again (salvation is an established fact); confession takes place only to keep the lines of communication open. Our guilt is often no more or less than our fear that if we do something bad, we will be kicked out. We falsely think that God is like our employer, teacher, or occasional friend. He isn't. He is the Father, and fathers (at least good ones) don't stop being fathers. Comparing earthly fathers to the heavenly Father, Jesus said, "If you then, being evil, know how to give good gifts to your children, how much more shall your Father who is in heaven give what is good to those who ask Him!" (Matt. 7:11).

Second, not only should you readjust your thinking if you are suffering from false guilt, but you also should reprogram your mind. I have just gotten into computers by using a word processor to write books and articles. (I have always felt guilty writing with anything but a quill pen, so it is a major step for me.) And I have learned something about the necessity of reprograming if the program in the computer is wrong. I believe that Christians have to do something like that with their minds.

Let me explain. Most of us feel we are controlled by our emotions. We think that if we don't feel like doing something, we can't do it. We think that if our feelings suggest something to our minds, the feelings must reflect reality. If there ever was a lie, a real whopper, that's it. Let me give you a principle that can change your life: your mind controls your emotions, and you control your mind. Feelings, emotions, and proclivities are not reality. Anyone who tells you different has lied to you.

As a pastor, I have performed hundreds of marriage ceremonies. Often I hear newly married parties say something like this: "I don't feel married." I often reply, "Stay with it a while.

It takes a bit of getting used to. Eventually the truth will sink in."

Now let's suppose a newly married couple doesn't take my advice and their feelings are more real to them than the fact that they're now married. Let's suppose, further, that every time they suspect they're married, they say to themselves, *I can't be married because I don't feel married.* Believe it or not, they are programing their minds in a certain way. I suppose that if they pushed it far enough and often enough, they would never think they are really married. If someone asked them if they are married, they would always reply, "No, we're not married." After a while, their feelings would become reality.

That's what a lot of Christians have done with their feelings of sin. First John 1:9 says, "If we confess our sins, He is faithful and righteous to forgive us our sins and to cleanse us from all unrighteousness." That's a fact. If you have confessed your sins, you are forgiven. If you don't feel forgiven, you are doing what our imaginary couple has done. You have simply denied the facts for your feelings. Whenever you feel guilty about something you have confessed, reprogram your mind. Say to yourself, "I have confessed that before God; He is not a liar; He has told me that I'm forgiven; therefore, I am forgiven. Anything other than that fact is a lie, and I will treat it like any other lie. I won't believe it." Then ask God to give you the grace to treat it as a lie.

Is this a magic formula? Of course not. It's a part of a process whereby gradually you learn to live your life by the facts and not by emotions. One day you will wake up and say, "I'm free! Praise God almighty, I'm free!"

And then one final word. If you suffer from false guilt, not only should you readjust and reprogram, but you also should review. Suffering from false guilt is one of the most subtle ways in which Satan goes after Christians. It's not a problem you deal with once and then it's over. When you least expect it, you'll find you have fallen into the sin of false guilt. And so a Christian needs to review God's grace constantly and praise Him for it.

Yesterday my wife and I worshiped at a church where a

friend of mine is the pastor. I had been feeling guilty about a number of things, and without my knowing it, I was walking around bearing false guilt. When we entered the sanctuary, I noticed that my friend's sermon was going to be about sin and forgiveness. I thought to myself, *I wish he would talk about something else. I already know all the things he is going to say.* As a matter of fact, I did know all the things my friend would teach that morning. But do you know what happened? As my friend taught the old truths from the Scriptures, I found myself free. I found the Holy Spirit once again applying the truth of Jesus and His love to my life. When I left that church, I felt like a new man.

No Christian knows the truth of God's grace so well that he or she doesn't have to hear it again and again. If you have a problem with false guilt, let me suggest that you review, memorize, and think about the great message of the Bible: you don't have to be guilty about the sin that Christ has already taken to the cross. You are forgiven.

In *Prime Rib and Apple*, Jill Briscoe has a great description of Eve's eating the forbidden fruit in the Garden of Eden. "Prime Rib [Eve] took the hand Omnipotence [God] had fashioned from her little piece of bone and plucked the piece of forbidden fruit. She placed it between the lips Omnipotence had framed to praise Him and absorbed into her system the poisons of independence, selfishness, and death. *And Jesus prepared to leave for Bethlehem.*"[4]

---

4. Jill Briscoe, *Prime Rib and Apple* (Grand Rapids: Zondervan Publishing House, 1976), p. 19.

10 A HERITAGE OF EXAMPLE

If Jesus has come...
I have a model.

For you have been called for this purpose, since Christ also suffered for you, leaving you an example for you to follow in His steps.
1 Peter 2:21

A number of years ago, I was part of a committee that invited some two hundred pastors from all over the United States to the Los Angeles area. The purpose of the meeting was to bring together pastors from different denominations and backgrounds. It was our hope that once they knew and trusted each other they would be able to unite against some of the problems facing our country. At one of the sessions during the conference, we divided the pastors into small groups. Each group was asked to discuss two questions and report back to the main body. The first question asked what the United States would be like if the whole country were permeated with the Spirit of Christ. The second question asked what we could do in our ministries to make what we had just described happen.

The results from each of the groups were interesting, and the answers to the questions were varied. But the most interesting response was to the second question. The topmost answer on every group's list was that our country has a desperate need for models of righteousness. In other words, it is terribly important that the world see us as the definition of Christian concepts.

When the world asks, "What's love?" it ought to be able to look at Christians and find the answer. When people want to know what it means to care, to be involved, to understand, they ought to be able to look at the lives of Christians and find a definition for the terms.

The Power of Example

The proposition of this chapter is that we can become models because we have a model. Our model is Jesus Christ. In John 13, Jesus gave a living illustration of service. He washed the disciples' feet and said, "You call Me Teacher and Lord; and you are right; for so I am. If I then, the Lord and the Teacher, washed your feet, you also ought to wash one another's feet. For I gave you an example that you also should do as I did to you" (John 13:13–15). In John 15:12, Jesus said, "This is My commandment, that you love one another, just as I have loved you."

When the Prince entered the hinterlands of the kingdom as a servant, He came to show His subjects how to live. Jesus came to die, but He also came to show *us* how to die; He came to love us, but He also came to show *us* how to love others; He came that we might be forgiven, but He also came that *we* might know how to forgive others. In other words, Jesus gave form to obedience.

I play golf, and I'm not very good at it. But I'm getting better. My improvement certainly hasn't come from reading books about golf, however. I've read a lot of them, and what they say sounds nice on paper. But when I put their tips into practice, they just don't work the way the books say they should. Instead, I have a friend who is an excellent golfer, and he has been taking me out on the course and giving me advice. Because he is showing me how to play better golf, I am playing better golf. The principle is this: an illustration is better than instruction. Maybe a better way to put it is that an illustration plus instruction is better than just instruction.

That is what the incarnation is all about. We knew what to

do, but now we know *how* to do it, because Jesus has shown us how.

Frustration in the Christian Life

I suspect that none of this is new to you. I suspect further that you have probably tried to follow Jesus' example for most of your Christian life but have had little success. After all, you aren't Jesus and you can't be expected to do what Jesus did. Right? Wrong! Jesus said, "Truly, truly, I say to you, he who believes in Me, the works that I do shall he do also; and greater works than these shall he do; because I go to the Father" (John 14:12). In other words, Jesus came to teach us how to walk in His ways *and do it successfully.*

If the thought of following Christ successfully frustrates you because you have tried so often and failed so miserably, let me welcome you to the club. There isn't a Christian alive who hasn't known that frustration—and I have felt it more than most.

It is my contention that Christians are frustrated in their obedience to Christ for two reasons. First, they are obedient to Him for the wrong reasons, and second, they misunderstand the example to which they are to be obedient. Let's deal with those problems in order.

Obedient for the Wrong Reasons

First, many of us try to be obedient to Christ in order to solicit God's love. In the last chapter, I spoke briefly about this problem, but now let's discuss it in more detail.

I have a friend who owns a candle factory, and when I visited the factory I got an education in how candles are made. In this particular candle factory, the workers are paid on the basis of "piece work." That means they are paid according to how many units they turn out rather than how many hours they work. It was amazing to see how fast those folks could turn out the boxes of candles. They were moving so fast I could hardly see their hands.

Many of us think that piece work is the way we ought to relate to God. His love and blessings are meted out to us on the basis of our volume of production. Some Christians are moving about as fast as the workers in that candle factory. If we can turn out just one more prayer, one more evangelistic encounter, one more rally, one more dollar for the kingdom, one more loving act, then God will notice and "up the pay."

Nothing, however, could be farther from the truth. In fact, that's the direction to total frustration. Let me remind you of 1 John 4:10: "In this is love, not that we loved God, but that He loved us and sent His Son to be the propitiation for our sins." In other words, God's love is not dependent on anything except God. His love isn't geared to our ability to earn it.

A man came into my study and said, "Pastor, if my daughter marries that—idiot, I'm going to disown her!"

Now, to be perfectly honest with you, I didn't like the young man much more than he did, but pastors don't express those kinds of views. So I said to him, "Sit down, Bill. You don't mean that. You love your daughter, and whatever she does, your love shouldn't change if it really is love."

One of the great doctrines of the Bible is called "the perseverance of the saints." The doctrine says that you don't hold God but that He holds you, and when you belong to Him you always will belong to Him, no matter what. The truth of that doctrine was one of the most wonderful discoveries of my life. I really wanted to please God, but I knew my own sin, and it scared me. So I held onto God until my knuckles were white. One day I just couldn't hold on any longer. I tried—I really tried, but I just couldn't do it anymore; so I let go, thinking I would fall into the abyss.

Do you know what happened? I didn't fall at all. In fact, I didn't even move. I found that He was holding onto me, and that was what really mattered. He told me, "I give eternal life to them, and they shall never perish; and no one shall snatch them out of My hand. My Father, who has given them to Me, is greater than all; and no one is able to snatch them out of the Father's hand" (John 10:28–29).

Paul was right:

> Who shall separate us from the love of Christ? Shall tribula-
> tion, or distress, or persecution, or famine, or nakedness, or peril,
> or sword?...But in all these things we overwhelmingly conquer
> through Him who loved us. For I am convinced that neither
> death, nor life, nor angels, nor principalities, nor things present,
> nor things to come, nor powers, nor height, nor depth, nor any
> other created thing, shall be able to separate us from the love of
> God, which is in Christ Jesus our Lord. (Rom. 8:35; 37-39)

If you are obedient because you want God to notice and then
love you because you are obedient, you not only are very frustrated, but you also are very foolish.

Second, a lot of Christians are obedient because they want to
help God out with His world. One of the most interesting religious developments of the fifties and early sixties was the
thought of Teilhard de Chardin, who mirrored the somewhat
earlier philosophy of Alfred North Whitehead. Both men saw
God as evolving with His creation: the creation is incomplete,
just as God is incomplete. But hang on, God, we're here! We're
working on it; we'll salvage the situation! And God reared back
and gave a great, big, ol' belly laugh (see Ps. 2:4).

I don't know about you, but I'm tired of the feeling that everything depends on me. As a matter of fact, everything doesn't
depend on me; everything depends on God, and He is perfectly
capable of running His universe.

> Thine, O LORD, is the greatness and the power and the glory
> and the victory and the majesty, indeed everything that is in the
> heavens and the earth; Thine is the dominion, O Lord, and Thou
> dost exalt Thyself as head over all. Both riches and honor come
> from Thee, and Thou dost rule over all, and in Thy hand is power
> and might; and it lies in Thy hand to make great, and to
> strengthen everyone. Now therefore, our God, we thank Thee,
> and praise Thy glorious name. (1 Chron. 29:11-13)

Have you noticed the modern proclivity to have systems? No
matter what you want to do, you can find a system that will en-
able you to do it. You can find a book on how to have a happy
life, how to pull your own strings, how to be number one, how
to intimidate, how to build a house, how to get rid of ugly fat,

and how to make a million without using any of your own money.

Christians suffer from the same proclivity. Someone has said that the chief end of man is to glorify God and to organize Him forever. Implicit in the Christian systems—ten steps to knowing God's will, four ways to save your marriage, God's design for a better relationship with your children—is the idea that if we do them right, we will be helping God bring the world around to His way of thinking. Sometimes systems can be helpful to us, but when they become "helpful" to God, they smell like smoke because they are from the pit of hell.

Listen! God doesn't need any help. When your obedience is geared to that goal, it is not only frustrating—it is silly.

Third, many of us make an effort at obedience because God is some kind of monster who must be placated with our obedience. Of course, we would never say so, but we really feel it in our heart of hearts. In *Eternity in Their Hearts*, Don Richardson gives ample evidence to counter the spurious view that our concept of God developed from polytheism to monotheism and from primitive to sophisticated forms. He shows that almost all peoples began with the idea of one God and that many of the primitive religions we study in high school and college are actually inferior forms of an earlier, more accurate and sophisticated religion. In other words, the animism and idol worship we see in a number of societies are usually not the beginning of the development to a monotheistic religion, but rather, the deterioration of an earlier belief in one God.

Richardson tells the fascinating story of Ethiopia's Gedeo people. Deep in the hill country of south-central Ethiopia, the Gedeo tribe worships and sacrifices to a god by the name of Sheit'an. Sheit'an is an evil, malevolent god who demands sacrifices from his worshipers. While they sacrifice to Sheit'an, they are aware of, though rarely pray to, another god by the name of Magano. Albert Brant, a missionary to the Gedeo tribe, asked them, "How is it that you regard Magano with profound awe, yet sacrifice to Sheit'an?"

They replied, "We sacrifice to Sheit'an, not because we love him, but because we simply do not enjoy close enough ties with

Magano to allow us to be done with Sheit'an."[1] Brant built on
their understanding and taught them that Magano's son died to
give them "close ties."

The point is this: the primitive Gedeo tribe is not as primitive as we would at first think, especially when we consider the
parallels among modern-day Christians. We have gods, too. We
talk about the God of love who sent His Son to die on a cross in
our place, and we worship another god who demands that we
sacrifice far more than what has already been sacrificed in
Christ. Our obedience comes from a need to placate the second
god so he won't be mad at us. We play Christian "games" in
which we do a "bad" thing today and think that we're okay because tomorrow we'll do a "good" thing and the scales will be
balanced. We are righteous and loving because if we aren't, the
second god we worship will strike us with a lightning bolt. Obedience given to satisfy a monster god is like a sacrifice offered to
the sun so it will come up in the morning. Our frustration is
magnified by such silly behavior.

The Right Reason to Obey

So, why be obedient? *Obedience is the response of a child who has
been loved.* Paul put it this way: "For the love of Christ controls
us" (2 Cor. 5:14a). In other words, obedience is the natural response of the heart to the reality of love.

In C. S. Lewis's *The Lion, the Witch and the Wardrobe*, the first
of *The Chronicles of Narnia*, two beavers told the children who had
wandered into the kingdom of Narnia about Aslan, Lewis's allegorical representation of Christ. Mr. Beaver said that when
Aslan came, he would make everything right and would correct
the considerable wrongs in Narnia. He said the children would
understand when they met him.

1. Don Richardson, *Eternity in Their Hearts* (Ventura: Regal Books, 1978), p. 54.

"But shall we see him?" asked Susan.

"Why, Daughter of Eve, that's what I brought you here for. I'm to lead you where you shall meet him," said Mr. Beaver.

"Is—is he a man?"asked Lucy.

"Aslan a man!" said Mr. Beaver sternly. "Certainly not. I tell you he is the King of the wood and the son of the great Emperor-Beyond-the-Sea. Don't you know who is the King of Beasts? Aslan is a lion—the lion, the great lion."

"Ooh!" said Susan. "I'd thought he was a man. Is he—quite safe? I shall feel rather nervous about meeting a lion."

"That you will, dearie, and no mistake," said Mrs. Beaver, "if there's anyone who can appear before Aslan without their knees knocking, they're either braver than most or else just silly."

"Then he isn't safe?" said Lucy.

"Safe?" said Mr. Beaver. "Don't you hear what Mrs. Beaver tells you? Who said anything about safe? 'Course he isn't safe. But he's good. He's the King, I tell you."[2]

The best theme throughout the seven chronicles is the developing love between the children and Aslan. It is not unlike the love that develops between Christ and the Christian.

Have you ever noticed how you want to please those who love you? My wife and I worked one summer after college with a summer camp for children. We had a group of four- to six-year-old boys in our cabin, and let me tell you, it was a growing experience. We learned lots of important lessons that summer (for example, don't feed little boys watermelon just before they go to bed), but the best lesson we learned was how children respond to love. My method of discipline had always been to "beat up" on kids until they do what's right. But in this particular camp, we were not allowed to raise a hand in violence to them. We had to learn some ingenious methods of dealing with the children as well as our own frustration.

My wife, Anna, was a natural. She just loved those little boys until they would do anything for her. One boy, the meanest five year old of the bunch, did everything in his power to test her love for eight weeks. I will never forget the last day of camp when he brought a bouquet of wild flowers to Anna. With

2. C. S. Lewis, *The Lion, the Witch and the Wardrobe* (New York: The MacMillan Company, 1969), p. 64.

tears streaming down his cheeks, he said, "Miss Anna, I don't want to go home, because nobody there loves me."

Our obedience is nothing more or less than the bouquet of flowers we give to someone who has loved us and demonstrated that love to us. In our obedience to God, we know He would never ask us to do anything that would be ultimately harmful to us. Because He loves us, we can trust Him with our obedience.

Jesus' Example Misunderstood

I suggested earlier that Christians are frustrated in their obedience because they obey Christ for the wrong reasons and because they have misunderstood Christ's example. Let's examine His example more closely.

Most of us think of Jesus' example as one of love, compassion, righteousness, and so on. There is some truth to that, but let me suggest that the real example Jesus gave us was not an example of action, but an example of being. That sounds kind of strange, so let me explain.

Jesus said, "If I do not do the works of my Father, do not believe Me; but if I do them, though you do not believe Me, believe the works, that you may know and understand that the Father is in Me, and I in the Father" (John 10:37–38). "He who believes in Me does not believe in Me, but in Him who sent Me. And he who beholds Me beholds the One who sent Me" (John 12:44–45).

John made an amazing statement in the first chapter of his gospel: "No man has seen God at any time; the only begotten God, who is in the bosom of the Father, He has explained Him" (John 1:18).

Jesus also said, "Truly, truly, I say to you, the Son can do nothing of Himself, unless it is something He sees the Father doing; for whatever the Father does, these things the Son also does in like manner. For the Father loves the Son, and shows Him all things that He Himself is doing" (John 5:19–20a). In Jesus' "High Priestly Prayer," He prayed,

> I do not ask in behalf of these alone, but for those also who believe in Me through their word; that they may all be one; even as

Thou, Father, art in Me, and I in Thee, that they also may be in Us; that the world may believe that Thou didst send Me. And the glory which Thou hast given Me I have given to them; that they may be one, just as We are one; I in them, and Thou in Me, that they may be perfected in unity, that the world may know that Thou didst send Me, and didst love them, even as Thou didst love Me. (John 17:20–23)

Paul wrote, "He is the image of the invisible God, the firstborn [i.e., unique] of all creation" (Col. 1:15).

Do you see it? The primary example Jesus gave us was not in what He did, but in who He was. In other words, it is not in His acting, but in His being. Did you ever think that all the miracles of Jesus can be duplicated and sometimes surpassed by God's servants in the Old Testament? Not only that, but He said Himself that His followers would do greater works than He did (see John 14:12).

The principal impact of the incarnation is not in what Jesus taught either. Everything Jesus taught can be found in the Old Testament. One of the great things happening in our time is the rediscovery of Jesus the Jew. He was, among other things, a Jewish rabbi who taught from the body of literature God had already revealed.

Nor was the primary impact of the incarnation of God in Christ in His goodness. Of course, Jesus had to be the perfect "lamb" in order to effect our salvation, but was it necessary that He provide an example of goodness? No, it was not. As a matter of fact, there were lots of examples of goodness God could have used. In 2 Kings 22:1–2, the Bible says, "Josiah was eight years old when he became king, and he reigned thirty-one years in Jerusalem; ... And he did right in the sight of the LORD and walked in the way of his father David, nor did he turn aside to the right or to the left." If God had needed an example of goodness, He could have used Josiah.

So what was the impact of the incarnation of God in Christ? Pay attention! *The primary impact of the incarnation of God in Christ is the incarnation of God in Christ.* "The Son can do nothing of Himself, unless it is something He sees the Father doing" (John 5:19). "My teaching is not mine, but His who sent me"

(John 7:16). "Now is the Son of Man glorified, and God is glorified in Him" (John 13:31).

Jesus was not obedient so He could become the Son of God. Rather, He was the Son of God, and was thereby obedient. He was not faithful in order to be God incarnate. He was God incarnate, and was therefore faithful. Arnold Lund put it this way: "There is no market for sermons on the text: God so loved the world that He inspired a certain Jew to inform His contemporaries that there was a great deal to be said for loving one's neighbors." No! God loved the world so much that He gave His Son!

A couple of years ago, I was teaching at a conference where two years before I had met a man I loved. Have you ever "clicked" with someone you met for the first time? Something happened and you knew you were going to be good friends for the rest of your lives. Well, the man I met at this conference was like that. In the few short days we were together, we developed a great and deep friendship. Between the time I met him and the time I went back to speak for the same conference two years later, my friend went home to be with the Lord. So I went to this particular conference with a good deal of sadness, because I knew my friend would not be there.

After the first evening session, a young man came down the aisle of the church and asked if he could speak with me.

"Sure you can," I replied. "And by the way, I knew your father and I loved him."

The young man was shocked. "How did you know who I am?" he asked.

"Are you kidding?" I said. "You smile like your father, you walk like your father, you part your hair like your father, and you talk like your father. You couldn't be anybody else."

Now let me ask you something about that boy. Do you think he stood in front of the mirror each morning and practiced walking like his father? Of course not. Do you think he worked for hours to get his hair to part like his father's? Do you think he worked with a tape recorder until he could sound just like his father? Of course not. He walked, talked, and looked like his father because he was his father's son. He didn't have to imitate—he just had to be.

Jesus was His Father's Son. He didn't come to show us how to speak Hebrew or wear a beard. His example was being, not acting. I heard two Christians talking not too long ago, one older and mature and the other a new believer. The older Christian was berating the new Christian because the new Christian had gone to a dance. The "spiritually mature" woman ended her lecture with these words: "My dear, can you imagine Jesus' going to a dance?"

The young woman thought for a moment and then said without any rancor, "No, I can't. But I can't imagine His flying in an airplane, either." Out of the mouth of babes! She was beginning to understand the example Jesus gave us. Jesus didn't come to act out a play where He made a point to act in certain ways. Jesus came simply to be who He was. His example was primarily one of being and not one of acting.

Following Jesus' Example

Now here comes the important part. The *Christian life*, following Christ's example, is not so much a life of acting but of being. Christians are called to abide in Christ in exactly the same way Christ abides in the Father. Jesus said, "Abide in Me, and I in you. As the branch cannot bear fruit of itself, unless it abides in the vine, so neither can you, unless you abide in Me. I am the vine, you are the branches; he who abides in Me, and I in him, he bears much fruit; for apart from Me you can do nothing" (John 15:4–5). Remember His prayer in John 17: "I do not ask in behalf of these alone, but for those also who believe in Me through their word; that they may all be one even as Thou, Father, art in Me, and I in Thee, that they also may be in Us." The form of obedience Jesus has given to us is abiding in Him, as He is abiding in the Father.

"What a strange-looking cow," said the man from the city to his farmer cousin. "Why doesn't that cow have any horns?"

"Well, you see," explained the country boy, "some cows are

born without horns and never had any, and others shed theirs, and some we dehorn, and some breeds aren't supposed to have horns at all. There are lots of reasons why some cows ain't got horns. But the reason that cow ain't got horns is that it ain't a cow, it's a horse."

There are lots of Christians who are trying their best to follow the example of Christ in all they do. And do you know the result? They are simply tired. They are like horses trying to pretend they're cows. It has been said so many times that it has become a cliché, but its truth has made it a cliché: the Christian life isn't difficult, it is impossible. It has only been lived by one person, and that person is Jesus Christ. If it is lived by you, it will only be because Jesus Christ lives it through you.

It is amazing to me the length to which Christians will go to get away from the principle that the Christian life means abiding in Christ in the same way Christ abides in the Father. When their Christian lives have lost their power, they go to conferences on how to have spiritual power. They think that when they are not experiencing normal Christian lives, what they need to do is read the Bible a little more, pray a little more, and go to church one more time each week and everything will be fine. Well, it won't, and it won't because that is not the way God ordained for us to walk with Him. He sent His Son to reconcile us to Himself and to give us an example of how to turn salvation into sanctification.

So often I have felt the way John Michael Talbot felt as he wrote in his spiritual journal, *Changes*:

> But I must also say I am wearied by a fellowship of many words. I grow tired of talking about the worship. I would much rather simply worship. I grow tired of talking about music. I would much rather simply make music. I grow tired of talking about humility and love. I would rather simply serve in humility and love. I grow tired of talking about "being" a Christian. I would much rather just "be."[3]

3. John Michael Talbot, *Changes, a Spiritual Journal* (New York: Crossroad, 1984), p. 60.

In one of his great classics, *The Pursuit of God*, A. W. Tozer made the same point:

> Every age has its own characteristics. Right now we are in an age of religious complexity. The simplicity which is in Christ is rarely found among us. In its stead are programs, methods, organizations and a world of nervous activities which occupy time and attention but can never satisfy the longing of the heart. The shallowness of our inner experience, the hollowness of our worship, and that servile imitation of the world which marks our promotional methods all testify that we, in this day, know God only imperfectly, and the peace of God scarcely at all.[4]

If you want to be obedient to God, abide in Christ. Don't go on a pilgrimage to the Holy Land; don't do something religious like getting baptized in water shipped directly from the river Jordan; and don't wear another religious trinket or read another religious book (except, of course, this one). Listen, if you want to be obedient to God, get close to Jesus. The Bible says, "This is the work of God, that you believe in [cleave to, trust, rely on, have faith in, lean on] Him whom He has sent" (John 6:29).

Now, if you are like me and most Christians, you want me to give you a system whereby you can abide in Christ. But systems are for computers, not people. I can give you some principles (and I'm going to do that in a minute), but knowing Christ and abiding in Him aren't done with a system any more than knowing and abiding in your wife or your friend are accomplished by following a system. The Greek word for *abide* means abide. And so, to abide in Christ is simply to stay close to Him through His Word and His presence. It means you have to give time to the effort. It means you have to exclude other things. It means you simply have to stay close to Him.

Principle No. 1: Abiding in Christ is an act of faith. Paul said, "As you therefore have received Christ Jesus the Lord, so walk in him" (Col. 2:6). How did you receive Christ? You did it by faith. You knew you were a sinner, someone told you about

4. A.W. Tozer, *The Pursuit of God* (Wheaton: Tyndale House, 1982), p. 17–18.

Him, and you rejoiced in the good news that He would accept you on the basis of His vicarious death on the cross. Paul said that in the same way you received Him, you must walk in Him. How? By faith.

Let me suggest a little prayer for you to pray similar to the one you probably prayed when you became a Christian. "Father, You have told me that I am to abide in Christ. You made it a commandment, and therefore I know it is Your will that I abide in Him. Grant me the grace to follow Your will, and I accept in faith that I now abide in Him." That prayer is an expression of faith and acceptance of His will that you abide in Christ.

Principle No. 2: Abiding in Christ is an act of time. We want everything yesterday. Someone told me recently of a cartoon in which a cannibal was shaking the contents of a box into a boiling pot. The box had written on it, "Instant Missionary." We want everything instantly, and hardly anything worth anything comes instantly. It took time for you to develop your really close friendships. A good marriage doesn't just happen after you say "I do." A good marriage takes years to develop. The same is true for a relationship with Christ.

Principle No. 3: Abiding in Christ is an act of utilizing the means of grace He has given. You can't abide with someone without talking to him, listening to him, or being a friend to his friends. The same is true for Christ. Prayer, Scriptures, and fellowship are essential tools for being with Christ.

Principle No. 4: Abiding in Christ is an act of just being with someone. I am only now learning to move from the silence of my relationship with Christ. I don't know about you, but I have a tendency to think that reality is found in what I do; so my prayer life is more doing than anything else. I pray for two or three hundred people each morning, and when I finish praying for them and talk to Christ, I usually just blither before Him. Sometimes I feel He is saying to me, "Just be quiet. Just stop talking. Just be still for a change and let's be together." I am learning to do that, and the more I just silently meditate on His Person, His love, and His grace, the more I become like Him.

Someone has said that hurry isn't from the devil, hurry *is* the devil. That's very true in my life. I need to stop doing things and start just being with the One who (much to my amazement) wants just to be with me. I believe Christ would like to speak to us in the silence, but we are so busy talking and doing that we can never hear Him. Someone tells about an archbishop who went to the cathedral to have his evening devotions. He knelt before the chancel steps and prayed in a loud voice, "O Lord Christ."

A voice echoed from heaven, "Yes, child."

They found the archbishop the next morning dead from a heart attack caused by shock. But we ought to be surprised when God *doesn't* speak, not when He does.

Here is the point: growth comes from abiding in Christ in the same way He was abiding in the Father. We don't abide in Him by growing. That is why so many of us are so frustrated in our walk with Christ. A dog doesn't bark to become a dog; a dog barks because he *is* a dog. Just so, a Christian doesn't do good things in order to be a Christian. A Christian does good things because he is a Christian. Stay close to Christ, and you will be surprised at the growth you will have because you were close to Him. His gift to you for just *being* with Him is that He will make you more and more like Him. Love, joy, peace, patience, kindness, goodness, faithfulness, gentleness, and self-control (see Gal. 5:22) are not the things you do in order to abide in Christ's Spirit. They are the fruit that comes *from* abiding in Christ's Spirit.

When Charles Kingsley was asked the secret of his productive life, he didn't write a book on how to be successful. He simply smiled and, referring to F. D. Maurice, said, "I had a friend." That's it. That's the secret, and you should not let its simplicity fool you. Obedience has form, and that form is Jesus Christ. When people see what He has done in your life, simply smile and say, "I have a friend who loves me and will love me forever."

11 A HERITAGE OF POWER

If Jesus has come...
I'm in with the kingdom's King.

*For He delivered us from the domain of darkness, and transferred us to
the kingdom of His beloved Son.*

Colossians 1:13

I'm writing these words the morning after the night before.
The Republican National Convention ended last night, and
now that both major parties in the United States have finished
their conventions, the campaign will swing into high gear. I
watched both the Democratic and Republican conventions on
television, and I must say, I found myself having very strong
feelings about many of the issues addressed by both parties.
There were times when I felt proud to be an American, and
other times when I was ashamed. I cheered my candidates,
thrilled to their speeches, and winced when a reporter said
something negative about them. I found myself so involved
with the political speeches and the debates that I fell into the
trap of thinking the outcome of the world depended on the outcome of the election. I was so emotionally involved that I found
myself thinking, *If so-and-so is not elected, our country is in terrible
trouble. In fact, given the positions taken by the other candidate, I wonder
if we would even survive.*

But now it is the morning after the night before, and I'm
feeling better. I might even get well. This morning, after all the
politics, I'm thinking like a Christian again, and I have remembered the truth that God is sovereign and is in charge. I've re-

membered the truth about the parties, the speeches, the flags, the noise, the promises, the institutions, the money, the hype. It's all going to pass away, and none of it will be of any use except as the God of the universe decides to use it. It's sort of like watching an old movie on television when you realize that everybody in it is dead. When my head cleared this morning, I remembered that the ultimate fate of the United States, and indeed the whole world, is not dependent on the Republicans or the Democrats, the communists or the capitalists, the conservatives or the liberals. The ultimate fate of the world is dependent on God.

When the former Archbishop of Canterbury, Geoffrey Fisher, visited Jerusalem, he accomplished what was almost impossible: he received the unanimous praise of all the religious factions in the Holy City. As if that were not enough, he then went to Istanbul, where he received a royal welcome from the Ecumenical Patriarch. From there Fisher went to Rome, where he was received with open arms by Pope John. Then Archbishop Fisher returned home, where he was met by a crowd of reporters.

One of the reporters asked the Archbishop what his most memorable experience was while on his history-making journey. He thought for a moment and said, "My most memorable experience was of a camel that looked at me with ineffable scorn." Maybe that camel knew something others had forgotten. "Remember Him before the silver cord is broken and the golden bowl is crushed, the pitcher by the well is shattered and the wheel at the cistern is crushed; then the dust will return to the earth as it was, and the spirit will return to God who gave it. 'Vanity of vanities,' says the Preacher, 'all is vanity!' " (Eccles. 12:6–8).

Have you ever noticed that history has a way of reversing the decisions and observations of the present? Our problem is that we make value judgments on the basis of incomplete data, and thus we place too much value on political elections and ecclesiastical journeys. I am not saying, of course, that these things are unimportant, but perhaps the camel had the right idea. Perhaps this year's election and the unity of the relgious leaders won't even be footnotes in the history books of the future.

If you had been present at the trial of Jesus before Pilate, the Roman procurator of Judea, Samaria, and Idumea, you would not have bet a nickel for Jesus of Nazareth. He was standing trial before the real power brokers of the world. The ecclesiastical power of the priests, the political power of the procurator, and the military power of the soldiers all seemed formidable when placed next to the wandering carpenter from Nazareth. But history has reversed the judgment and we know the truth: nobody would even know about Pilate, the priests, or the soldiers had they not had their encounter with the carpenter.

It was an interesting trial. If you had been there, the words of Jesus would have seemed strange, the delusions of a deranged mind. Pilate faced the carpenter. A cynical smile crossed Pilate's face as he stifled a yawn. He asked Jesus if He really was the king of the Jews.

> Jesus answered, "Are you saying this on your own initiative, or did others tell you about Me?"
> Pilate answered, "I am not a Jew, am I? Your own nation and the chief priests delivered You up to me; what have You done?"
> Jesus answered, "My kingdom is not of this world. If My kingdom were of this world, then My servants would be fighting, that I might not be delivered up to the Jews; but as it is, My kingdom is not of this realm."
> Pilate therefore said to Him, "So You are a king?"
> Jesus answered, "You say correctly that I am a king. For this I have been born, and for this I have come into the world, to bear witness to the truth. Every one who is of the truth hears My voice." (John 18:34–37)

And so the claim is made. Don Quixote? Maybe so and maybe not; nevertheless, the claim is there for all to hear and to decide.

The Choice

Apparently Pilate had started a custom on the Passover of releasing one political prisoner to the people as a gesture of benevolence. On this occasion, he offered a choice: Jesus or Barabbas. The Scripture says in Luke 23:19 that Barabbas had been thrown in prison for a civil insurrection and for murder. But the crowd chose Barabbas over Jesus.

Let me tell you something I'll bet you didn't know about Barabbas. His name was possibly a messianic title: *Bar* meaning "son of" and *Abbas* meaning "the father." There is a tradition that says Barabbas's given name was Jesus. Thus you have a man named Jesus Barabbas. And then note the way Pilate refers to Jesus in Matthew 27:22: "Then what shall I do with Jesus *who is called Christ?*" Why add "who is called" unless there was another Jesus present?

Some scholars believe Barabbas was one of a number of false messiahs who were in Jerusalem and its environs during the time of Jesus. Looking to the prophecies of the Old Testament referring to a military and political leader, Barabbas's leadership was one of violence, force, manipulation, and intimidation. Jesus' leadership was one of meekness, love, gentleness, and persuasion. Pilate gave the crowd a choice between Jesus Barabbas and Jesus Christ, and they chose the former because Barabbas understood the political realities of the world.

Almost two thousand years have come and gone, and people are still faced with that choice. We choose between Jesus Barabbas and Jesus Christ. They can't both be king; one is right and one is wrong. And most people are still choosing Jesus Barabbas because they honestly can't see the reality of the kingdom ruled by Jesus Christ.

I have a friend who says that every time the government hugs the church, the church hugs back. He's right, and that fact worries me, because when you embrace the ways of Barabbas's kingdom—when you use the language of Barabbas's kingdom, when you learn the techniques of Barabbas's kingdom, when you accept the rewards of Barabbas's kingdom, and when you nod too much in the direction of Barabbas's kingdom—you are a part of Barabbas's kingdom. (If it walks like a duck, quacks like a duck, and looks like a duck, it probably *is* a duck.)

Jesus said, "Enter by the narrow gate; for the gate is wide, and the way is broad that leads to destruction, and many are those who enter by it. For the gate is small, and the way is narrow that leads to life, and few are those who find it. Beware of the false prophets, who come to you in sheep's clothing, but inwardly are ravenous wolves" (Matt. 7:13–15).

And so the kingdom of Jesus is not always popular. Sometimes it seems to be lost in the shuffle, but it is the only kingdom of any importance, and in the end, when God turns the last page of history, the announcement will be made: "Now the salvation, and the power, and the kingdom of our God and the authority of His Christ have come" (Rev. 12:10).

When Rome was finally invaded in A.D. 410, some Romans tried to blame the Christians. It was a natural, though spurious, assertion given the fact that Emperor Theodosius had made Christianity the official state religion. Fifteen years after his death, Rome fell, adding fuel to the contention that Christians were somehow responsible. Augustine was brought into the controversy through some correspondence with two Roman officials about the relationship between the church and Rome. Out of those reflections, he wrote *The City of God*. The opening section of that work is bold in its assertions:

> The glorious city of God is my theme in this work, which you, my dearest son Marcellinus, suggested, and which is due to you by my promise. I have undertaken its defense against those who prefer their own gods to the Founder of this city—a city surpassing glorious, whether we view it as it still lives by faith in this fleeting course of time, and sojourns as a stranger in the midst of the ungodly, or as it shall dwell in the fixed stability of its eternal seat, which it now with patience waits for, expecting until "righteousness shall return to judgment," and it obtain, by virtue of its excellence, final victory and perfect peace.[1]

---

1. Augustine, *The City of God*, Great Books of the Western World, vol. 18, Robert Hutchins, ed. (Chicago: Encyclopaedia Britannica, 1952), p. 129.

The Kingdom of God

The biblical doctrine of the kingdom of God is fraught with theological controversy. Although the purpose of this book is not to resolve it (even if I could), there are many questions about the kingdom of God about which Christians are in wide agreement. Let it be sufficient to say in passing that the kingdom of God has two realities, one in the present and another in the future. Paul said, "For He delivered us from the domain of darkness, and transferred us to the kingdom of His beloved Son" (Col. 1:13). That is the present reality, and if you are a Christian you are a part of the present kingdom of God. Jesus said that when we pray we should pray, "Father, hallowed be Thy name. Thy kingdom come..." (Luke 11:2). That is the future reality of the coming kingdom, and if you are a Christian you will continue to be a part of it then.

Now let me give you some facts about the kingdom of God that you ought to remember when you are deciding between the kingdom of Barabbas and the kingdom of Jesus. When Jesus came, we had an opportunity to see Him as either a wandering Nazarene carpenter or the King. If He is only a carpenter, then Jesus Barabbas's kingdom is the only legitimate one. Sometimes it will succeed and sometimes it will fail, but it is the only kingdom. On the other hand, if Jesus was the King, then your knee should be bowing before Him at this very moment. At any rate, consider the following facts, and you will never be able to say that nobody told you.

Fact No. 1: The kingdom's beginning was small. Jesus said in Matthew 13:31–32, "The kingdom of heaven is like a mustard seed, which a man took and sowed in his field; and this is smaller than all other seeds; but when it is full grown, it is larger than the garden plants, and becomes a tree, so that the birds of the air come and nest in its branches."

One of the great mistakes people make is the mistake of despising small beginnings. The works of Christ's kingdom have always had small beginnings. Christ is King of the Jews, and they started small. Nobody will deny that Abraham was a small beginning.

> Now the Lord said to Abram, "Go forth from your country, and from your relatives and from your father's house, to the land which I will show you; and I will make you a great nation, and I will bless you, and make your name great; and so you shall be a blessing; and I will bless those who bless you, and the one who curses you I will curse. And in you all the families of the earth shall be blessed." (Gen. 12:1-4)

Abraham was just a nobody God chose to use in creating the kingdom. You wouldn't have chosen him in a million years—but be careful that you don't despise small beginnings.

Bethlehem was a small beginning. Who would have thought that the King would come through Bethlehem? And the King's disciples? How would you like to have been on the personnel committee deciding on the King's court? Peter? James? John? Judas? You've got to be kidding! The kingdom had a small beginning, but don't let it fool you.

To ensure that his son would be the heir of his kingdom, a king once required his nobles to swear allegiance to his son while he was only an infant. They laughed and refused, but the king changed their minds with these words: "Gentlemen, he is little now, but he *will* grow." Sometimes things of great import and worth begin very small—things as small and insignificant as a group of wandering Jews in the middle of the desert, a prophet from the hill country of Tekoa, or a carpenter behind a bench in Nazareth. Beware of small beginnings; they have a tendency to grow.

Fact No. 2: The kingdom's operation is often secret. You don't ever see a mustard seed growing until it is out of the ground, and even then you might miss it. You turn around and say, "Wow, I never noticed that tree before." You see a tree's growth only in retrospect by counting its rings.

I remember speaking at a missions conference for young people a number of years ago. I had a great sermon prepared on the mission enterprise of the church, but the leader came up to me right before speaking and said, "Steve, we have just found out that a lot of these kids aren't Christians. Would you present the gospel?" So instead of making my missions presentation, I presented the plan of salvation. At the end, I gave an invitation to those who had not come to Jesus Christ. Do you know what happened? Nothing. Not a soul stirred. I remember leaving the auditorium that night in shame. I could hardly wait to get on the airplane and head for home.

If you are a public speaker, you know how I felt. Every time I thought about that experience I blushed. I thought about how horribly I had presented Christ to those young people. I remembered my halting words and my poor illustrations, and I just wanted to die. I tried to forget about it by saying to myself, *These things happen; no big deal.* But it *was* a big deal, and every time I even heard the name of the town where I had given that presentation, I winced.

Let me tell you the rest of the story, however. Five years later, I was speaking at another conference, and a young man came up to me and said, "Mr. Brown, you don't know me, but a few years ago I was at a missions conference where you spoke." I thought, *God, what did I do to deserve this?* He went on. "The night you spoke, I received Christ, and now I'm a student in seminary and I'm going to be a pastor, and I just wanted to thank you. Not only that, but I've still got the tape of what you said that night, and I've shared it with my friends; I can't tell you how God has used your words." I thought, *Why didn't You tell me about this five years ago?* God was teaching me a lesson with that experience: you don't have to see the kingdom to get it to work. The kingdom operates in secret.

This is an important principle: if you have to hype your point, it probably isn't true or it isn't from God. Vance Havner said that Jesus performed miracles and didn't advertise, and we advertise miracles and don't perform them. He has a point. Most of the kingdom's important operations don't take place on television programs or in great crusades. They take place in people's hearts. But don't underestimate the kingdom because it operates in secret.

Fact No. 3: The kingdom's growth is slow. Again, in the case of the mustard seed, it grows to a tree very slowly. I don't know about you, but I'm impatient. When you watch the kingdom, however, you have to be patient. The kingdom grows, but it grows slowly. Sometimes it even seems to retreat; sometimes it seems to lie fallow; sometimes you hardly even notice it's growing. But don't be fooled. Slow growth is still growth, and Aesop was right about the tortoise and the hare.

When China was closed to missionaries, most Christians around the world were devastated. What would happen to the Christians in China? Could they stand the persecution? Would the church fall? I was in China recently, and do you know what has happened? The Christians who were left behind by the mis-. sionaries have been let loose. They are multiplying at a phenomenal rate. When the Bamboo Curtain fell, there were about one million Chinese believers. C. Peter Wagner tells what happened:

> The efforts made by the Communist government to extinguish the Church were massive. Pastors were jailed, Bibles were confiscated and burned, church buildings were closed, Bible schools were disbanded, Christian literature was outlawed, both lay leaders and clergy suffered humiliation, imprisonment, and torture, and most outside observers thought the Gang of Four and the Cultural Revolution would be successful in wiping out the Church. But as the bamboo curtain began to lift in the late seventies, and news began to filter out, it became clear that the Holy Spirit had remained behind in China and was doing mighty things. The first word was that the 1 million were still there. Then the estimates continually grew to 3 or 5 million, then 8 or 10 million and now even conservative estimates range between 30 and 50 million.[2]

How about that? The story can be repeated all over the world, from Africa to Korea, from India to Indonesia. On and on the growth continues like a small hole in a dam, and then another and another until there is no longer a barrier. Sometimes

2. C. Peter Wagner, *On the Crest of the Wave* (Ventura: Regal Books, 1983), p. 30.

the missionaries wanted to go home, to throw in the towel, to give up. But they didn't, because they knew about the kingdom; they knew that God works by process; and when God starts something, its slowness shouldn't be misjudged.

The Most Important Fact

I have given you these three facts first because I don't want you to find yourself confused by the world's evaluation of success. The kingdom of Christ is small, secret, and slow. But it *is* the kingdom of Christ—the Father gave it to Him (see Luke 22:29)—and His coming ensures that another fact, perhaps the most important one, is also true: the kingdom's completion is inevitable. In the second chapter of Philippians, the apostle Paul spoke of the amazing fact of the incarnation of God in Christ, and then he said something no one should ever forget: "Therefore also God highly exalted Him [Jesus], and bestowed on Him the name which is above every name, that at the name of Jesus every knee should bow, of those who are in heaven, and on earth, and under the earth, and that every tongue should confess that Jesus Christ is Lord, to the glory of God the Father" (Phil. 2:9–11).

When you are choosing between the kingdoms of Jesus Barabbas and Jesus Christ, remember that God has started something that can never be stopped. The kingdom has a King, and some day every knee will bow (the easy way or the hard way) and every tongue confess (the easy way or the hard way) that Jesus is the King.

Once I was flattered by an offer to pastor a very large church. I called a friend, the late Aiken Taylor, and asked him if I should consider the offer. Aiken was never one to hedge on what he thought, and he said, "Steve, are you crazy? That church is like a train. You don't change its direction, you just get on it!" The kingdom of Christ is just like that. You can watch the train go by, or you can get on it—but you can't stop it. And some day, God will even remove the option of getting on it. The passenger list will be closed because the destination will have been reached.

Concerns of the King

There is still one more question to consider: what is the kingdom's destination? In other words, what is the King going to do? Where is He going? What is the ultimate result of the present reality of the kingdom? As one of the subjects of the kingdom of Christ, let me answer that by discussing four major concerns of the King.

Concern for His Glory

The Prince's first concern is for His glory and the parallel concern for His Father's glory. In his high-priestly prayer, Jesus prayed two petitions that are of interest to this particular discussion. At the beginning of the prayer, He prayed, "Father, the hour has come; glorify Thy Son, that the Son may glorify Thee" (John 17:1). Then near the end of the prayer, He prayed, "Father, I desire that they also, whom Thou hast given Me, be with Me where I am, in order that they may behold My glory, which Thou hast given Me; for Thou didst love Me before the foundation of the world" (John 17:24).

The Hebrew word for "glory" is *kābôd*, translated *doxa* in the Greek New Testament, from which we get the English word *doxology*. The word literally means "to be heavy." It lends itself to the idea that glory is laden with riches, power, position, and worth. When a teenager says something is "heavy, man, *heavy*," he doesn't know it, but he's close to the biblical meaning of glory. When Jesus talked about the kingdom's glory, He was talking about the worth, praise, weight, dignity, power, and position it would receive.

Now the interesting thing in this context is that the whole reason for the creation of the world in general, and the creation of you in particular, is that God would be glorified. "For from Him and through Him and to Him are all things. To Him be the glory forever. Amen" (Rom. 11:36). At the announcement of the birth of the King, the multitude of angels praised God and said, "Glory to God in the highest" (Luke 2:14). Paul wrote to the Ephesians, "To Him [God] be the glory in the church and in Christ Jesus to all generations forever and ever. Amen" (Eph. 3:21). In Luke 2:20, after the shepherds beheld the Christ child, they returned home "glorifying and praising God." And then the culmination of the kingdom is coming, "And every created thing which is in heaven and on the earth and under the earth and on the sea, and all things in them, I heard saying, 'To Him who sits on the throne, and to the Lamb, be blessing and honor and glory and dominion forever and ever.' And the four living creatures kept saying, 'Amen.' And the elders fell down and worshipped" (Rev. 5:13–14).

Do you see it? It's the purpose of the kingdom that the King might be glorified. If you are looking forward to the future, that is what you are going to be doing. If you want to be present at the end, you will be praising the King.

In a very practical way, everything is fulfilled and better off when it is serving the purpose for which it was created. I never asked them, but I suspect a tree is fulfilled in growing limbs and leaves, a cat is happy catching mice, and a dog is happy chasing mail carriers. But you were created for the praise of the King's glory; and if you are not living a fulfilled and joyful life, you haven't found the secret: you can't glorify yourself and the King at the same time. The kingdom's purpose in its creation, its growth, and its end is that the King be glorified, and in His glorification His Son is glorified. Some day we are going to stand at the end of time, when the purpose of creation has been fulfilled, and we are going to look at Him and say to one another, "Isn't He something? Doesn't He shine? Isn't He wonderful?" Paul understood: "Whether, then, you eat or drink or whatever you do, do all to the glory of God" (1 Cor. 10:30).

Concern for His Subjects

You also ought to be aware of the King's concern for His subjects. Let me give you an amazing text: "So then let no one

boast in men. For all things belong to you, whether Paul or
Apollos or Cephas or the world or life or death or things present
or things to come; all things belong to you, and you belong to
Christ; and Christ belongs to God" (1 Cor. 3:21-23). Jesus
said, "And you are those who have stood by Me in My trials;
and just as My Father has granted Me a kingdom, I grant you
that you may eat and drink at My table in My kingdom, and
you will sit on thrones judging the twelve tribes of Israel" (Luke
22:28-30). Paul wrote, "...giving thanks to the Father, who
has qualified us to share in the inheritance of the saints in light.
For He delivered us from the domain of darkness, and transferred us to the kingdom of His beloved Son" (Col. 1:12-13).

In the kingdom's present reality, the King's subjects have
His full interest and love. An ambassador for England once
said, "I represent the greatest power on earth, and if I get into
trouble it is that power that will stand with me," and a Christian
can say the same about the kingdom he represents. No wonder
Paul said, "We are ambassadors for Christ" (2 Cor. 5:20) and
was secure in that fact.

One time George Washington was coming from his head-
quarters on a cold, snowy day. Nobody noticed as he watched a
corporal browbeat his men into building a breastwork of logs.
They tried and tried, but each time one of the logs fell into the
snow. At one point, when a heavy log fell, Washington ran up
and pushed with them until the log was in place. Washington
then turned to the corporal and said, "Why didn't you help
your men?"

"I didn't help them because I am the corporal," he answered.

"Indeed," replied Washington, throwing open his greatcoat
and showing his uniform, "I am only the commander-in-chief.
The next time you have a log too heavy for your men to lift, you
can send for me!"

In that respect, the King is like Washington. He is not just a
King who reigns over His subjects from afar. He is a king who
has come to share with us the hardship of the kingdom on earth.
He is a companion King, and that is no small thing.

Concern for His Enemies

Third, the King is concerned for His enemies. Paul said, "While we were enemies, we were reconciled to God through the death of His son" (Rom. 5:10a). In other words, if you are the enemy of the King, His offer of amnesty and acceptance is still available. James Buswell has said about the kingdom,

> In the sense of the loyal underground in time of war, believers are now said to be within the "kingdom" of Christ. There is this difference, of course, that in time of war the underground exists as such only because of the weakness of the government of the rightful king. The fact that Christ is not now actively governing this world and enforcing His law in all human affairs, is *not* based upon any weakness whatsoever in His government or in His powers but is solely based upon His grace and His longsuffering.[3]

However, with all of that being said, there is still more to be said. "Don't assume," said Queen Victoria to the Archbishop of Canterbury, "that because God does not balance His books every Thursday, that God does not balance His books." With all God's graciousness and love, the kingdom's open door should never cause anyone to presume. "Therefore having overlooked the times of ignorance, God is now declaring to men that all everywhere should repent, because He has fixed a day in which He will judge the world in righteousness through a Man whom He has appointed, having furnished proof to all men by raising Him from the dead" (Acts 17:30–31). In other words, only a very foolish person fools around with a sovereign King.

C. S. Lewis wrote,

> When any man comes into the presence of God he will find, whether he wishes it or not, that all those things which seemed to make him so different from the men of other times, or even from his earlier self, have fallen off him....Do not let us deceive ourselves. No possible complexity which we can give to our picture of the universe can hide us from God: There is no copse, no forest,

3. James Oliver Buswell, *A Systematic Theology of the Christian Religion*, vol. 2 (Grand Rapids: Zondervan Publishing House, 1962), p. 347.

no jungle thick enough to provide cover. We read in Revelation of Him that sat on the throne "from whose face the earth and heaven fled away." It may happen to any of us at any moment. In the twinkling of an eye, in a time too small to be measured, and in any place, all that seems to divide us from God can flee away, vanish leaving us naked before Him, like the first man, like the only man, as if nothing but He and I existed. And since that contact cannot be avoided for long, and since it means either bliss or horror, the business of life is to learn to like it. That is the first and great commandment.[4]

Now we have a choice of kingdoms to which we will belong. But the time will come when the opportunity to choose will be gone. It will be too late to plead mercy before the King.

Concern for His Ultimate Reign

Finally, you ought to note the King's concern for His ultimate reign. Jesus said,

> But immediately after the tribulation of those days the sun will be darkened, and the moon will not give its light, and the stars will fall from the sky, and the powers of the heavens will be shaken, and then the sign of the Son of Man will appear in the sky, and then all the tribes of earth will mourn, and they will see the Son of Man coming on the clouds of the sky with power and great glory. (Matt. 24:29–30)

Jesus has already been given all power and authority in the world (see Matt. 28:18), but because of His patience and kindness, His hand is restrained. Peter said, "The Lord is not slow about His promise, as some count slowness, but is patient toward you, not wishing for any to perish but for all to come to repentance. But the day of the Lord will come like a thief" (2 Pet. 3:9–10a).

Jesus said that the kingdom could be compared to a field in which a farmer had sowed good seed. While the farmer was

4. C. S. Lewis, *God in the Dock* (Grand Rapids: William B. Eerdmans Publishing Company, 1970), p. 47.

asleep, an enemy came and sowed some weeds in the same field. When the seeds began to grow, the weeds were intermingled with the wheat and the field was a mess. When the slaves saw what had happened, they told the farmer and suggested that they pull the weeds.

> But he said, "No; lest while you are gathering up the tares, you may root up the wheat with them. Allow both to grow together until the harvest; and in the time of the harvest I will say to the reapers, 'First gather up the tares and bind them in bundles to burn them up; but gather the wheat into my barn.' " (Matt. 13:29–30)

If I were not a subject of the King, I would be terribly afraid. But for those of us who serve the King, the kingdom's message is one of great joy and comfort. Malcolm Muggeridge wrote, "As Christians we know that here we have no continuing city, that crowns roll in the dust and every earthly kingdom must sometime flounder, whereas we acknowledge a king men did not crown and cannot dethrone, as we are citizens of a city of God they did not build and cannot destroy."[5]

Jesus told us to pray, "Thy kingdom come. Thy will be done, on earth as it is in heaven" (Matt. 6:10). Some day that prayer will be gloriously answered. Some day He will return. Some day the King will claim His total sovereign rule. Some day a trumpet will sound, and we who belong to the King will look up, and it will begin. "These will wage war against the Lamb, and the Lamb will overcome them, because He is Lord of lords and King of kings, and those who are with Him are the called and chosen and faithful" (Rev. 17:14).

Those are the facts, and I have given them to you as honestly as I know how so you can choose between the kingdom of Jesus Barabbas and the kingdom of Jesus Christ. Whether you believe the facts is of little importance, because belief is irrelevant to facts.

5. Malcolm Muggeridge, *The End of Christendom* (Grand Rapids: William B. Eerdmans Publishing Company, 1980), p. 52.

Someone told me recently about two pastors who were conducting a funeral together. One pastor was to read the Scripture and lead a prayer, at which time the other pastor was to give the eulogy. As the prayer was coming to a conclusion, the pastor who was to give the eulogy realized he had left his notes in his study two floors above the chapel where the funeral was taking place. He slipped up behind the pastor who was praying and whispered in his ear, "I'm leaving. Keep praying until I get back." The prayer was one of the longest in the history of that particular church, but eventually the pastor who had forgotten his notes found them and returned to the pulpit to deliver a successful eulogy.

I have often thought about that humorous incident and the pastor's words, "Keep praying until I get back." Jesus said the same thing to us. He said, "I'll be back; you keep on praying until I return. Stay faithful and keep on keeping on until I get there." It's scary sometimes because you don't know when He's coming and you're not sure how much longer you can keep on keeping on.

Don't worry. It won't be so long that you'll have to give up. He promised. He said He'd be back. You can hang your hat on that.

I just thought you ought to know.